AF182613

SpringerBriefs in Business

For further volumes:
http://www.springer.com/series/8860

G. Tomas M. Hult

Boundary-Spanning Marketing Organization

A Theory and Insights from 31 Organization Theories

Springer

G. Tomas M. Hult
Michigan State University
East Lansing
USA

ISSN 2191-5482 ISSN 2191-5490 (electronic)
ISBN 978-1-4614-3818-2 ISBN 978-1-4614-3819-9 (eBook)
DOI 10.1007/978-1-4614-3819-9
Springer New York Heidelberg Dordrecht London

Library of Congress Control Number: 2012936827

This volume is adapted, by permission of the Academy of Marketing Science, from the article, "Toward a theory of the boundary-spanning marketing organization and insights from thirty-one organizational theories," by G. Tomas M. Hult, Journal of the Academy of Marketing Science (2011), 39:509-536, © Academy of Marketing Science 2011

Printed on acid-free paper

Springer is part of Springer Science+Business Media (www.springer.com)

Preface

Now more than ever, marketing has a key boundary-spanning role—a role that has also redefined the composition of the marketing organization. In this SpringerBrief, the marketing organization's integrative and mutually reinforcing components of marketing activities, customer value-creating processes, networks, and stakeholders are delineated within their boundary-spanning roles as a particular emphasis—labeled "marketing organization theory" or abbreviated as MOR to capture the first letter of "marketing" and the first two letters of "organization." This SpringerBrief builds on and is an extended and more elaborate version of Hult (2011), also published in a Springer publication (*Journal of the Academy of Marketing Science*). Thematic marketing insights from a collection of 31 organization theories are used to advance knowledge on the boundary-spanning marketing organization within four areas: strategic marketing resources, marketing leadership and decision-making, network alliances and collaborations, and the domestic and global marketplaces.

An abbreviated version of this SpringerBrief was originally published in the "organization theory" special issue of the *Journal of the Academy of Marketing Science* (vol. 39, No. 4, 2011). I am grateful to the Academy of Marketing Science for permission to use the original version of the article as the basis for this significantly extended and to some degree revised version of the theory of the boundary-spanning marketing organization. I appreciate the input provided by David J. Ketchen, Jr. (coeditor for the special issue of *JAMS* on organization theory) and O.C. Ferrell (vice president of publications for the Academy of Marketing Science). Informal and formal feedback from Ulf Andersson, Artur Baldauf, Roger Calantone, George Day, Cornelia Dröge, Nicolai Foss, Bruce Lamont, Ahmet Kirca, Jeannette Mena, Neil Morgan, Tom Murtha, Torben Pedersen, Stan Slater, and Doug Vorhies helped crystallize my thoughts regarding the composition of the MOR theory and the use of the large set of organization theories that helped inform work on the boundary-spanning marketing organization.

East Lansing, MI, USA G. Tomas M. Hult, PhD

Contents

Chapter 1
Introduction

Research on the role of marketing in organizations has typically adopted either a functional or a cross-functional perspective. Moorman and Rust (1999, p. 181) describe a functional marketing organization as having "the concentration of the responsibility for marketing activities (knowledge and skills) within a group of specialists in the organization." Workman et al. (1998, p. 32) defines "cross-functional dispersion of marketing activities as the extent to which functional groups, other than marketing, are involved in traditional marketing activities." While there has been a tendency in the marketing literature in the last 2 decades to increasingly emphasize the cross-functional perspective over the functional perspective (Moorman and Rust 1999), each perspective and its potential combinative effects (Kogut and Zander 1992) has key implications for the marketing organization (Workman et al. 1998). More importantly, each perspective is rooted in the idea of a set of marketing *activities* being performed by marketing specialists and/or nonspecialists.

> The boundary-spanning marketing organization is defined as an entity encompassing marketing activities that cross a firm's internal and external customer value–creating business processes and networks for the purposes of satisfying the needs and wants of important stakeholders.

The boundary-spanning marketing organization is set apart from traditional organizations, which have more clearly defined boundaries, markets, and/or hierarchies (cf. Thorelli 1986; Williamson 1975). These boundary-spanning activities, rooted in an organization's capabilities (Day 1994), are implemented within customer value-creating processes (Srivastava et al. 1999), which are embedded in networks (Achrol and Kotler 1999) to benefit stakeholders (Freeman 1984). There is a natural complexity inherent in the interdependencies in this form of an organization, but there is also strong potential for superior rewards (i.e., organizational performance) from operating a well-functioning boundary-spanning marketing organization (cf. Thompson 1967). Importantly, marketing activities that are tied to a function or department (Moorman and Rust 1999) are as important as those that

G.T.M. Hult, *Boundary-Spanning Marketing Organization: A Theory and Insights from 31 Organization Theories*, SpringerBriefs in Business 20,
DOI 10.1007/978-1-4614-3819-9_1, © Academy of Marketing Science 2011

are cross-functional, or both, within the boundary-spanning marketing organization (Workman et al. 1998). The descriptions of the main constructs in this research are summarized in Table 1.1.

Table 1.1 Descriptions of the main constructs

- *Marketing activities*. Marketing activities are created and performed as a direct functioning of an organization's (superior) capabilities (Day 1994) and take place in customer value-creating processes (Srivastava et al. 1999) and networks (Achrol and Kotler 1999; Anderson et al. 1994; Johanson and Vahlne 2011). For example, "capabilities are manifested in such typical business activities as order fulfillment, new product development, and service delivery" (Day 1994, p. 38). In fact, there are a plethora of marketing activities that stem from marketing-based capabilities (e.g., Day 1994; Vorhies and Morgan 2005)
  - *Responsive marketing activities*. Responsive marketing activities "is the attempt to understand and satisfy customers' [and other stakeholders'] expressed needs" (Narver et al. 2000, p. 8). Expressed needs are defined as "the needs of a customer [and other stakeholders] of which the customer [stakeholder] is aware and, therefore, can express" (Narver et al. 2000, p. 7)
  - *Proactive marketing activities*. Proactive marketing activities "is the attempt to understand and satisfy customers' [and other stakeholders'] latent needs" (Narver et al. 2000, p. 8). Latent needs are defined as "needs of which the customer [stakeholder] is unaware" (Narver et al. 2000, p. 7)
  - *Inside-out activities*. Rooted in Day's (1994) work on marketing capabilities, inside-out activities refer to the notion that "there is a recognition that sensing and scanning [activities] should emphasize the need to" (Day 2011, p. 187) "define managerial traits, management systems, and organizational designs that will keep the organization alert to opportunities and threats, enable it to execute on new opportunities, and then constantly morph to stay on top" (Teece 2010, p. 206). "These actions are initiated by mindful scanning activities mounted by the firm" (Day 2011, p. 187). As such, inside-out activities are "activated by market requirements, competitive challenges, and external opportunities" (Day 1994, p. 41)
  - *Outside-in activities*. Rooted in Day's (1994) work on marketing capabilities, outside-in activities (as opposed to inside-out activities) begin "with the market" (Day 2011, p. 187). "The management team steps outside the boundaries and constraints of the company as it is and looks first to the market; How and why are customers changing? What new needs do they have? What can we do to solve their problems…?" (Day 2011, p. 187). As such, for outside-in activities "the focal point is almost exclusively outside the organization … to connect the processes that define the other organizational capabilities to the external environment and enable the business to compete by anticipating market requirements ahead of competitors and creating durable relationships with customers, channel members, and suppliers" (Day 1994, p. 41)
  - *Boundary-spanning activities*. "Spanning capabilities are exercised through the sequences of activities that comprise the processes used to satisfy the anticipated needs of customers by the outside-in capabilities and meet the commitments that have been made to enhance relationships" (Day 1994, p. 42)
  - *Cultural competitiveness*. "The degree to which [organizations] are predisposed to detect and fill gaps between what the market desires and what is currently … this predisposition can arise when [organizational] members develop shared values and beliefs centered on the importance of serving the market offered" (Hult et al. 2002, p. 577)

(continued)

Table 1.1 (continued)

- *Customer value-creating processes*. "Customer value creation necessitates the accomplishment of three central organizational tasks: The development of new customer solutions and/or the reinvigoration of existing solutions; continual enhancement of the acquisition of inputs and their transformation into desired customer outputs; and the creation and leveraging of linkages and relationships to external marketplace entities, especially channels and end users" (Srivastava et al. 1999, p. 169)
  - *Product development management processes*. These processes "aim to create solutions that customers need and want" (Srivastava et al. 1999, p. 169)
  - *Supply chain management processes*. These processes incorporate "acquisition of all physical (and increasingly informational) inputs, as well as the efficiency and effectiveness with which they are transformed into customer solutions" (Srivastava et al. 1999, p. 169). A more elaborate definition, based on the CSCMP, is included in the paper in the SCM section
  - *Customer relationship management processes*. These processes address "all aspects of identifying customers, creating customer knowledge, building customer relationships, and shaping their perceptions of the organization and its products" (Srivastava et al. 1999, p. 169)
  - *Complementary effects*. In its most simplistic form, the logic is as follows. Take the basic formula of $A+B \rightarrow C$. When tested together, both A and B positively affect C. However, if the test entailed $A \rightarrow C$ and $B \rightarrow C$ in two simplistic regression models and neither A nor B significantly affected C, then we can argue that "complementarity" exists between A and B. Specifically, A and B are significant only if tested jointly on C. This is different from combinative effects in that the Kogut and Zander (1992) theorizing would require the product of A and B to also be significant (i.e., $A+B+A^*B \rightarrow C$, where each of A, B, and A*B significantly affects C)
  - *Combinative effects*. "What firms do better than markets is the sharing and transfer of the knowledge of individuals and groups within organizations" (Kogut and Zander 1992, p. 383). The logic is that creating new knowledge does not occur independent from the firm's current capabilities. Instead, new knowledge is a function of a firm's "combinative capabilities" to generate new applications, views, and innovations from existing (but often scattered) knowledge. In that sense, combinative capabilities refer to the "intersection of the capability of the firm to exploit its knowledge and the unexplored potential of the technology" (Kogut and Zander 1992, p. 391)
- *Networks*. Achrol and Kotler (1999, p. 148) define a network organization as "an independent coalition of task- or skill-specialized economic entities (independent firms or autonomous organizational units) that operates without hierarchical control but is embedded, by dense lateral connections, mutuality, and reciprocity, in a shared value system that defines 'membership' roles and responsibilities"
  - *Actors in the network*. The actors in the network control activities and resources; individuals, groups of individuals, parts of firms, and groups of firms, for example, can be actors (Håkansson and Johanson 1984; Håkansson and Östberg 1975)
  - *Activity links in the network*. An activity occurs when one or several actors combines, develops, exchanges, or creates resources by utilizing other resources (cf. Hunt 2000). Activities performed within a unit are typically called "production activities," and activities performed between units are typically called "exchange activities" within the network perspective (e.g., Håkansson 1989)
  - *Resource ties in the network*. The resource ties represent a necessary condition for all intra-unit activities (Håkansson 1989; Pfeffer and Salancik 1978; Thompson 1967). In the case of the individual units within network(s), five types of resources can be identified (Håkansson 1989, 1992; Waluszewski 1989), each related to some parts of the corporate environment: input goods, financial capital, technology, personnel, and marketing (cf. Barney 1991; Wernerfelt 1984)

(continued)

Table 1.1 (continued)

- ◦ *Internal networks*. Internal networks "are designed to reduce hierarchy and open firms to their environments" (Achrol and Kotler 1999, p. 148)
- ◦ *Vertical networks*. Vertical networks "maximize the productivity of serially dependent functions by creating partnerships among independent skill-specialized firms" (Achrol and Kotler 1999, p. 148)
- ◦ *Intermarket networks*. Intermarket networks "seek to leverage horizontal synergies across industries" (Achrol and Kotler 1999, p. 148)
- ◦ *Opportunity networks*. Opportunity networks "are organized around customer needs and market opportunities and designed to search for the best solutions to them" (Achrol and Kotler 1999, p. 148)

- *Stakeholders*. Freeman (1984, p. 46) defines stakeholders as "any group or individual who can affect or is affected by the achievement of the organization's objectives." Stakeholders are categorized into two core groups: primary and secondary (Clarkson 1995; Hult et al. 2011)
  - ◦ *Primary stakeholders*. Primary stakeholders are those on whom the marketing organization depends for its survival (i.e., shareholders, employees, customers, suppliers, regulators, and local communities) (e.g., Hult et al. 2011)
  - ◦ *Secondary stakeholders*. Secondary stakeholders (e.g., special interest groups, competitors, trade associations, mass media, and social media) do not have a strong or direct tie to the marketing organization, cannot exercise any legal authority over the organization, and are not vital for its survival (e.g., Eesley and Lenox 2006; Hult et al. 2011)

The success of the boundary-spanning marketing organization depends on how well the marketing activities, customer value-creating business processes, networks, and stakeholder focus are molded together to form an integrated organization. In addition, based on the integration of 31 organization theories (a listing of the 31 organization theories used in the study can be found in Table 1.2), four "strength" characteristics emerge as important for the functioning of the organization. Specifically, developing an appropriate level of (1) strength in the organization's strategic marketing resources, (2) strength in the organization's marketing leadership and decision-making, (3) strength in the organization's network alliances and collaborations, and (4) strength in the organization's marketplace operations (e.g., segmentation, targeting) that are imperative to achieve sustainable superior performance.

I continue the SpringerBrief by delineating a theory of the boundary-spanning marketing organization (abbreviated MOR theory), followed by elaborating on the knowledge that can be derived from 31 organization theories for this form of organization. The specific purposes of the SpringerBrief are (1) to theoretically describe and holistically integrate the components of the boundary-spanning marketing organization, (2) to encapsulate the original scope of 31 essential organization theories and describe their marketing scope and insights, and (3) to use the collection of the 31 organization theories to advance the knowledge on the boundary-spanning marketing organization.

The motivation for the SpringerBrief stems from three main areas. First, marketing organizations are no longer defined within traditional boundaries (e.g., departments, functions), markets, or hierarchies, and so a new conceptualization of the

Table 1.2 An alphabetical listing of the 31 organization theories

Adjustment-cost theory of the firm
Agency theory
Behavioral theory of the firm
Bounded rationality theory
Competence-based theory
Contingency theory
Eclectic theory of international production
Game theory
Industrial organization
Information economics theory
Institutional theory
Knowledge-based view of the firm
Network theory
Organizational ecology
Prospect theory
Real options theory
Resource-advantage theory
Resource-based view of the firm
Resource dependence theory
Service-dominant logic
Signaling theory
Social capital theory
Stakeholder theory
Strategic choice theory
Systems theory
Theory of competitive rationality
Theory of multimarket competition
Theory of the growth of the firm
Theory of the multinational enterprise
Transaction cost economics
Upper echelons theory

marketing organization is needed to advance knowledge. Second, significant advances can be made by integrating organization theories, beyond a unique and sometimes narrow focus on just one theory as the theoretical underpinning. Third, the SpringerBrief significantly extends Hult (2011), an article which was part of the special issue of the *Journal of the Academy of Marketing Science* on "organization theory." A more in-depth coverage of the components of the boundary-spanning marketing organization (marketing activities, customer value-creating processes, networks, and stakeholders) is now included along with a more elaborate discussion of the 31 organization theories and a more intricate discussion of insights throughout. As such, the SpringerBrief serves as both an extended, new take on organization theory within marketing (via its delineation of the boundary-spanning marketing organization) and an extensive literature integration of 31 potentially valuable organization theories for the study of marketing thought.

Chapter 2
A Theory of the Boundary-Spanning Marketing Organization

The theory of the firm (Coase 1937) provides the theoretical underpinnings for the firm as an integrated and defined unit based on four basic themes: (1) the reason for the existence of the firm, (2) the logical boundaries of the firm, (3) the organization of the firm, and (4) the heterogeneity of the firm's actions. For example, the basic issues regarding the firm's existence include: why do firms emerge, and why are not all transactions mediated by the marketplace? Boundary issues include: why is the boundary between the firm and the marketplace defined as it is (which transactions should reasonably be performed internally, and which should be performed externally)? The notion of the firm's organization addresses: why are firms structured in a boundary-defining way, and what are the roles of formal and informal relationships? The heterogeneity of the firm captures questions such as: what drives the actions by the firm and the firm's resulting performance?

An earlier parallel to these boundary-defining themes of a firm can be found in works on "The Principles of Scientific Management" (Taylor 1911) and "Administrative Theory" (Fayol 1916). Administrative theory, similar to its near-contemporary the "Scientific Management" approach, is founded on the notion that firms are rational and closed systems. The firm was assumed to have clear objectives and relatively defined structural boundaries. The interactions of the firm with its environment and any other factors which are external to the firm were systematically ignored. Times have changed, and these changes have significant implications for a theory of the boundary-spanning marketing organization (i.e., MOR theory). Marketing is no longer confined to a department or a function (Workman et al. 1998).

Keith (1960, pp. 36–38) introduced this evolution of marketing about half a century ago by focusing on the "marketing company … [where] marketing permeates the entire organization," suggesting "we are moving from a company which has the marketing concept to a marketing company." A marketing organization is unique in that marketing is not attached to a department or function (e.g., Walker and Ruekert 1987) but is instead based on a set of activities (e.g., Day 1994). Emphasizing marketing activities instead of the marketing function allows marketing to permeate the entire organization (Homburg and Pflesser 2000) and serves to fuse together the

G.T.M. Hult, *Boundary-Spanning Marketing Organization: A Theory and Insights from 31 Organization Theories*, SpringerBriefs in Business 20,
DOI 10.1007/978-1-4614-3819-9_2, © Academy of Marketing Science 2011

"network of specialized organizations [that have become] the organizations of the future" (Achrol 1991, p. 78). These marketing activities have specific emphases depending on their internal–external focus. Day (1994) categorizes capabilities-based marketing activities at a coarse-grained level into inside-out (e.g., integrated logistics), outside-in (e.g., market sensing), and boundary spanning (e.g., strategy development). In addition, Vorhies and Morgan (2005) provide a compilation of some key marketing activities at a fine-grained level (e.g., pricing, product development, channel management, marketing communications, selling, marketing planning, marketing implementation).

Contemporary forms of vertically disaggregated marketing organizations, akin to sophisticated supply chain networks (i.e., complex webs of interdependent supply chains involving relatively autonomous organizations; Hult et al. 2004), are quasi entities involved in complex multilateral systems of activities. While traditional firms develop products through markets or hierarchies (Williamson 1975), the marketing organization model of MOR theory not only allows for control in the making of the product (i.e., hierarchy), similar to a vertically integrated firm, but it also allows for the flexibility associated with the buy model (i.e., markets) (cf. Thorelli 1986). As such, MOR theory captures the advantages of both markets and hierarchies while steering clear of many of the risks of each. In alignment with these thoughts, Moorman and Rust (1999) suggest that organizations are shifting away from functional marketing to a "marketing process organization" (i.e., an organization which disperses activities across non-specialists; Workman et al. 1998).

The historical foundation for such a theory of the marketing (process) organization can be partially traced to supply chains and the sales-marketing interface (e.g., Lusch et al. 2010; Malshe and Sohi 2009; Mentzer and Gundlach 2010; Stock et al. 2010). For example, Henry Ford's supply chain was composed of a vertically integrated collection of wholly owned vendors that supplied materials to Ford's production and assembly facilities. Likewise, rooted in the notion of having minimal inventories, Toyota developed its Kanban system in the 1970s with the goal of reducing waste by reducing inventory-carrying costs. The just-in-time concept of Kanban led many firms to also implement frequent deliveries of quality materials from firms in relatively close proximity to the assembly plant. The successive marketing systems adopted by many firms (e.g., Wal-Mart) included the development of integrative systems capabilities, at the point-of-sale and throughout the supply chain system, to have real-time data on what items to reorder (cf. Scheer et al. 2010). More recent examples include outsourcing and offshoring, along with establishing small business federations, as a way to capture the advantages of both markets and hierarchies while reducing the risks associated with each. The contemporary versions of these business models are held together by boundary-spanning marketing activities that facilitate managing the processes within and across the firm's boundaries and supply chain networks.

In support of the centrality of activities holding together the elements of the marketing organization, Webster (1992, 2009) and Day (1994) emphasize the importance of marketing activities as fundamental to cross-functional business processes, as do Vargo and Lusch (2004, p. 10) in their discussion of "process management."

Based on Srivastava et al. (1999, p. 169), marketing is composed of three primary customer value-creating processes: product development management (PDM; creating solutions the customer wants), supply chain management (SCM; acquiring physical and informational inputs and transforming them into customer solutions), and customer relationship management (CRM; identifying customers, creating customer knowledge, building customer relationships, and shaping customer perceptions) (cf. Luo 2010). In each of these processes, "marketing … infuses a customer orientation into the subprocesses … through the medium of individual marketing tasks," which are "defined broadly as specific items of work that marketing professionals typically do" (Srivastava et al. 1999, p. 172). The end result is that the core customer value-creating processes of PDM, SCM, and CRM—in a direct or interactive way—affect the financial performance of the firm (Ramaswami et al. 2009).

The three customer value-creating processes are embedded in networks of activity links, actors, and resources ties (e.g., Anderson et al. 1994; Johanson and Vahlne 2011). Early on, "these networks consisted of informal social ties, more a collection of dyadic bonds than a formal network, and functioned in the shadows of the formal organization" (Achrol and Kotler 1999, p. 147). However, the marketplace is increasingly driven by influential and often large-scale networks (Thorelli 1986). No longer are the social structures of networks the main focus for research and practice. Instead, networks are now formal governance structures that embody an alternative to Williamson's (1975) markets and hierarchy choices (Achrol and Kotler 1999). In fact, "the entire economy may be viewed as a network of organizations with a vast hierarchy of subordinate, criss-crossing networks" (Thorelli 1986, p. 38). Importantly, networks are not the same as administered markets (Williamson 1975), since a network may encompass only a small portion of one of several markets.

Based on Achrol and Kotler (1999, p. 148), four primary categories of network organizations can be embedded in MOR theory: "internal networks that are designed to reduce hierarchy and open firms to their environments; vertical networks that maximize the productivity of serially dependent functions by creating partnerships among independent skill-specialized firms; intermarket networks that seek to leverage horizontal synergies across industries; and opportunity networks that are organized around customer needs and market opportunities and designed to search for the best solution to them." Inherent in MOR theory, a marketing organization can be proficient and have experience with each of these four network models. However, the likely scenario is that a truly efficient marketing organization emphasizes one or a small set of network types at any given time to achieve superior performance.

Layered together, a focus on marketing activities (e.g., Day 1994) within the structure of the core customer value-creating processes of PDM, CRM, and SCM (Srivastava et al. 1999) at the level of the complexity inherent in the four categories of network arrangements (Achrol and Kotler 1999) makes up the main pillars of MOR theory. However, within the depiction of the activities, processes, and networks the marketing organization also adopts a stakeholder focus as an important component (e.g., Donaldson and Preston 1995; Mitchell et al. 1997). That is, a theory of the boundary-spanning marketing organization places emphasis on multiple

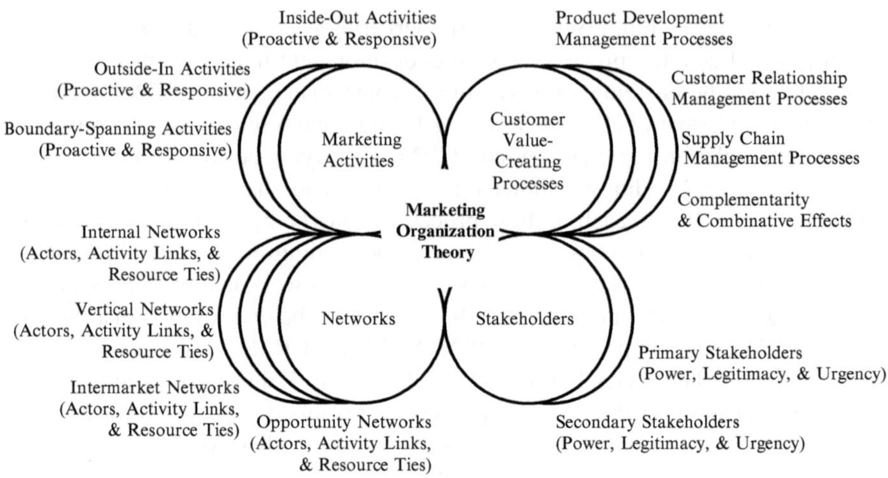

Fig. 2.1 The integrated elements of the boundary-spanning marketing organization

"actors" (i.e., stakeholders). Clarkson (1995) identifies these stakeholders as either primary (i.e., those that are crucial for the firm's survival and continued market success) or secondary (i.e., those that are not vital for the firm's survival but can still mobilize public opinion in favor of or against a firm). Primary stakeholders include customers, employees, suppliers, shareholders, communities, and regulators, while secondary stakeholders can be groups such as the media and special interest groups (e.g., Hult et al. 2011). In focus, now are actors involved in performing marketing activities in the firm's customer value-creating processes and those involved in the (multiple) network(s) of the firm. Overall, the boundary-spanning marketing organization encompasses an integrated foundation of (1) marketing activities (inside-out, outside-in, and boundary spanning), (2) customer value-creating processes (PDM, CRM, and SCM), (3) networks (internal, vertical, intermarket, and opportunistic), and (4) stakeholders (primary and secondary).

Figure 2.1 provides a depiction of the basic elements of MOR theory. Overall, the skeleton for this form of organization is built around a primary objective to develop and implement marketing activities within customer value-creating processes and to be a mechanism that fuses together these activities with the networks (including key actors) in which the firm is embedded in the marketplace. Ultimately, implications of MOR theory span both structural and behavioral marketing organization variables (cf. Olson et al. 2005). Significant overlaps exist in theoretical boundaries across the four elements of the boundary-spanning marketing organization. First, the central focus on marketing *activities* is also central to the behaviors exemplified in the core value-creating processes of PDM, CRM, and SCM as well as the activity links within the network focus. Second, a primary/secondary stakeholder focus is, in this case, synonymous with the focus on various "actors" included in the network. The remaining factor across the four elements of the marketing organization is "resource ties." Resources, in general, are viewed as critical across activities, processes, and networks—with boundary-spanning marketing organizations uniquely integrating their strategic resources to leverage a competitive advantage in the marketplace.

Marketing Activities

The fundamental premise for MOR theory rests on the notion that "marketing activities," rather than a focus on the marketing department or the marketing function, represent the central feature of contemporary marketing. Marketing activities are created and performed as a direct functioning of an organization's (superior) capabilities (Day 1994) and take place in customer value-creating processes (Srivastava et al. 1999) and networks (Achrol and Kotler 1999; Anderson et al. 1994; Johanson and Vahlne 2011). For example, "capabilities are manifested in such typical business activities as order fulfillment, new product development, and service delivery" (Day 1994, p. 38). In fact, there are a plethora of marketing activities that stem from marketing-based capabilities (e.g., Day 1994; Vorhies and Morgan 2005). The foundation for the development and implementation of these marketing activities permeates the fabric of boundary-spanning marketing organizations, beyond the marketing department and the marketing function.

Day (1994, p. 41) identifies three categories of capabilities manifested in marketing activities—"inside-out" (internal), "outside-in" (external), and "boundary-spanning"—as the broad categories of relevant activities for market-driven organizations. Examples of inside-out capabilities encompass financial management, cost control, technology development, integrated logistics, manufacturing/transformation processes, human resource management, and environment health and safety. Outside-in capabilities include market sensing, customer linking, channel bonding, and technology monitoring. Boundary-spanning capabilities encompass customer order fulfillment, pricing, purchasing, customer service delivery, new product/service development, and strategy development.

This collection of internal, external, and boundary-spanning marketing capabilities makes marketing's role in the organization (Moorman and Rust 1999) and society (Wilkie and Moore 1999) complex, integrative, and critically important. Given that these capabilities are manifested in activities, the marketing activities define the scope of the boundary-spanning marketing organization. As such, the focus on marketing activities is more critical in the formulation of the boundary-spanning marketing organization than are other influences (e.g., environment, industry) and/or elements (e.g., strategy, structure). And, importantly, the marketing activities are derived from inside-out, outside-in, and boundary-spanning marketing capabilities rather than from the scope inherent in a marketing department or the traditional marketing function (cf. Day 2011).

Also important is that today these activities do not "look like the product, place, price, and promotion activities enshrined in decades of textbooks" (Day 2011, p. 192).

While the so-called 4Ps of product, place, price, and promotion remain relevant, the boundary-spanning marketing organization will likely thrive on activities that are closely tied to its components of customer value-creating processes, networks, and stakeholders. In that spirit, I will briefly discuss a limited set of marketing activities that are, on a relative scale, critically important for the development, implementation, and maintenance of an effective and efficient boundary-spanning marketing organization in the subsequent sections on customer value-creating processes, networks, and stakeholders. However, it is important first to distinguish between responsive and proactive marketing activities (e.g., Atuahene-Gima et al. 2005; Blocker et al. 2011; Narver et al. 2000; 2004; Tsai et al. 2008) as they pertain to the outside-in, inside-out, and boundary-spanning marketing activities (e.g., Day 1994, 2011). In addition, I have included a brief section on "Cultural Competitiveness" (e.g., Hult et al. 2002) to focus attention on the fact that all marketing activities are not weighted equally.

Responsive Marketing Activities

Responsive marketing activities are "the attempt to understand and satisfy customers' [and other stakeholders'] expressed needs" (Narver et al. 2000, p. 8). Expressed needs are defined as "the needs of a customer [and other stakeholders] of which the customer [stakeholder] is aware and, therefore, can express" (Narver et al. 2000, p. 7). The stream of research on responsive (sometimes labeled reactive) market orientation and the marketing activities aligned with that market orientation is really what the marketing field largely called "market orientation" between 1990 (e.g., Kohli and Jaworski 1990; Narver and Slater 1990) and until 2000. Using the logic by Narver et al. (2000, p. 4), this form of "reactive" market orientation has also been referred to as "customer-led" (Slater and Narver 1998) and "customer-compelled" (Day 1999). In 2000, Narver et al. (2000, p. 7) introduced the idea of a "total market orientation" and broke the constructs of market orientation into two: "reactive market orientation" (later referred to as "responsive market orientation"; e.g., Narver et al. 2004, p. 334) and "proactive market orientation."

Proactive Marketing Activities

Proactive marketing activities are "the attempt to understand and satisfy customers' [and other stakeholders'] latent [and future] needs" (Narver et al. 2000, p. 8). Latent needs are defined as "needs of which the customer [stakeholder] is unaware" (Narver et al. 2000, p. 7). Building on the research by Narver et al. (2000), Slater et al. (e.g., Atuahene-Gima et al. 2005; Blocker et al. 2011; Narver et al. 2004) and some others (e.g., Tsai et al. 2008) have begun to focus increased attention on being proactive in the marketplace. Their specific emphasis is on proactive market orientation activities including, for example: helping "customers anticipate developments in their markets"; discovering "additional needs of our customers"; and searching for "opportunities in areas where customers have a difficult time expressing their needs" (Narver et al. 2000, p. 29). Narver et al. (2004, p. 334), in a directly connected article to their 2000 MSI working paper, focus on "responsive and proactive market orientation and new-product success." Atuahene-Gima et al. (2005, p. 464) focus on "the contingent value of responsive and proactive market orientations for new product program performance." Tsai et al. (2008, p. 884) focus on "the curvilinear relationships between responsive and proactive market orientations and new product performance." And, in the most recent article on proactive activities, Blocker et al. (2011, p. 216) focus on "proactive customer orientation [activities] and its role for creating customer value."

Overall, this research stream on organizations' need to be proactive and responsive stresses the need to also be proactive and responsive in terms of the inside-out, outside-in, and boundary-spanning marketing activities in the boundary-spanning marketing organization. A dedicated focus on outside-in and boundary-spanning activities, per Day's (1994, 2011) work, at least implies a need to be proactive. Likewise, it is important to be proactive in terms of "looking inward" to overcome what Day (2011, p. 187) refers to as the premature "myopically" narrowing and anchoring of the dialogue regarding marketing activities.

Cultural Competitiveness

Cultural competitiveness refers to "the degree to which [organizations] are predisposed to detect and fill gaps between what the market desires and what is currently offered … this predisposition can arise when [organizational] members develop shared values and beliefs centered on the importance of serving the market offered" (Hult et al. 2002, p. 577). Using the logic provided by Hult et al. (2002), the focus on the cultural competitiveness of boundary-spanning marketing organizations is not intended to suggest that such organizations possess cultures whose arrays of characteristics parallel those of more traditional organizational cultures. Accordingly, for members in boundary-spanning marketing organizations, especially when going beyond the boundaries of the traditional organization and involving so-called external value-chain members, "only certain cultural elements closely related to serving the market, such as competitiveness" (Hult et al. 2002, p. 577), are the critical ones in affecting marketing activities (e.g., Hult and Ketchen 2001; Hult et al. 2007b). Hult and collegues (Hult and Ketchen 2001; Hult et al. 2002, 2003b, 2007b) have addressed cultural competitiveness (also called "culture of competitiveness"; Hult et al. 2007b, p. 1035) in a number of studies. The key aspect of this research is that certain marketing activities pertaining to, in particular, stressing phenomena such as market orientation, entrepreneurship, innovativeness, and organizational learning make organizations more prone to exemplifying characteristics of a cultural competitiveness in their dealings with the marketplace. Such cultural competitiveness is important as an anchoring in boundary-spanning marketing organizations as they prioritize certain marketing activities to develop and implement over others in order to have a competitive advantage and achieve superior performance.

Customer Value-Creating Processes

Srivastava et al. (1999, p. 169) identify a set of three core business processes that specifically "contributes to customer value creation." These processes are: (1) PDM, (2) CRM, and (3) SCM. The PDM process is the most internally oriented of the three business processes and involves creating and developing products that satisfy the wants and/or needs of customers (Brown and Eisenhardt 1995). The CRM process is the most externally focused business process (cf. Aurier and N'Goala 2010) and "addresses all aspects of identifying customers, creating customer knowledge, building customer relationships, and shaping the perceptions of the organization and its products" (Srivastava et al. 1999, p. 169; cf. Reimann et al. 2010). The SCM process is boundary spanning given the integrated engagement of internal and external actors of the firm. "SCM encompasses the planning and management of all activities involved in sourcing and procurement, conversion, and all logistics management activities" (Mentzer and Gundlach 2010, p. 1; cf. Li et al. 2010).

The internal (i.e., NPD), external (i.e., CRM), and boundary-spanning (i.e., SCM) focus of the three customer value-creating processes as proposed by Srivastava et al. (1999) are remarkably similar in focus to Day's (1994, p. 41) "outside-in processes" (external emphasis), "inside-out processes" (internal emphasis), and "spanning processes." The capabilities associated with each process were briefly mentioned earlier in the "Marketing Activities" section. However, it is important to note that there is a high degree of alignment between Day's (1994) and Srivastava et al.'s (1999) work. The labeling is somewhat different, and Srivastava et al. (1999) certainly narrows the scope of the internal, external, and boundary-spanning focus by selecting NPD, CRM, and SCM as the capabilities that would tackle the processes initially described by Day (1994). In addition, Day's (1994) focus was largely on classifying capabilities into these three "buckets" of important customer value-creating processes. At the same time, neither Day (1994) nor Srivastava et al. (1999) place any real emphasis on the "marketing activities" associated with the "capabilities" in the case of Day (1994) and the "core business processes" in the case of Srivastava et al. (1999). Bringing it "down" to the activities level is important since marketing activities are at the center of the boundary-spanning marketing organization and what makes it thrive (and also what makes market-driven organizations and the core business processes thrive).

Each of the three customer value-creating processes is macro-oriented and subsumes a number of subprocesses (see Table 1 in Srivastava et al. 1999). For example, NPD involves such subprocesses as "ascertaining new customer needs" and "coordinating product design activities to speed up business processes" (Srivastava et al. 1999, p. 170). CRM involves such subprocesses as "identifying potential new customers" and "determining the needs of existing and potential new customers" (Srivastava et al. 1999, p. 170). SCM involves, for example, subprocesses such as "selecting and qualifying desired suppliers" and "managing (multiple) channels" (Srivastava et al. 1999, p. 170).

Collectively, the three processes are interconnected in terms of (macro and micro) interactions and interrelationships, and they are intended to be value creating in the marketing organization (cf. Esper et al. 2010). As such, both complementarity (cf. Hess and Rothearmel 2011; Richey et al. 2010) and combinative effects (Kogut and Zander 1992) are involved in the dynamics of the knowledge-intensive and customer value-creating processes. A key feature of these processes is also their close "linkages between individual marketing activities" and "those people [i.e., actors] charged with implementing them" (Srivastava et al. 1999, p. 169–170). To synthesize ideas of customer value-creating processes within the scope of MOR theory, activities and actors in the boundary-spanning marketing organization bind together (1) PDM processes, (2) SCM processes, and (3) CRM processes. Importantly, complementarity (dependence) and combinative effects (synergy) exist among these customer–value-creating processes.

Product Development Management Processes

Product development, as viewed within the notion of customer value-creating processes, has been centered in a skewed way on "new" product development. For example, Srivastava et al. (1999) list six subprocesses of PDM processes, and the top three are focused on something "new" (i.e., ascertaining new customer needs; designing tentative new product solutions; developing new solution prototypes). This is not to say that Srivastava et al. do not place some emphasis on the other aspects of product development, but the literature appears to have grabbed a hold of the new product aspect much more so than PDM processes in general. In this context, the notion of "innovation" has also been placed in the forefront; new products often, if not always require innovation of some form. However, even innovation can take on various forms (e.g., Hurley and Hult 1998).

Innovation can be of the form of product innovation, process innovation, administrative innovation, innovativeness of the organization's culture, and innovativeness in the fabric of the firm's various corporate units (e.g., SBUs), strategic groups, industry, country, etc. (cf. Short et al. 2007). Importantly, innovative firms are not always good at new product development, and having an innovative culture is not necessarily the same as being entrepreneurial (cf. Hult et al. 2003b) in taking advantage of the innovative new product or service developed (Hult and Ketchen 2001; Hult et al. 2002, 2007b; Hurley and Hult 1998). This of course begs the question: If you have an innovative culture and innovative strategy, do you have a more innovative product at the end than if you have just an innovative culture or an innovative strategy? And, if you can have only one, which is better to have: an innovative culture or an innovative strategy? The answers are intriguing and worthwhile to research, but the main story on NPD in the context of the boundary-spanning marketing organization is that NPD includes development of products that are "new-to-the-world" products, new product lines, line extensions, and product modifications. Only the "new-to-the-world" product category would be truly "new" in this context, and such a newness focus is too limiting for the NPD scope as a part of the customer value-creating processes Srivastava et al. (1999) describe as the three core business processes.

Supply Chain Management Processes

SCM processes related to marketing have often centered on the so-called marketing channels aspect of marketing (cf. Chabowski et al. 2011). In the past, logistics was also more front and center in marketing (e.g., Mentzer et al. 2001) until it (to some degree) broke off as a separate field with the founding of the National Council of Physical Distribution Management in 1963 (the organization's name changed to the Council of Logistics Management in 1985 and again to the Council of Supply Chain Management Professionals (CSCMP) in 2005). Interestingly, with the much more integrative work done in SCM, marketing along with many of its closely related fields has become more focused on SCM in the last decade (e.g., Boyer and Hult 2005a, b, 2006; Mentzer and Gundlach 2010).

The concept of SCM, originally recognized in the 1980s (Mentzer and Gundlach 2010), now spans the main areas of logistics (Hult et al. 2007a; Mentzer et al. 2001), supply management (i.e., sourcing purchasing, procurement; Hult 1998; Hult and Chabowski 2008; Hult et al. 2000), operations (e.g., Hult et al. 2010), and marketing channels. However, many more aspects of SCM cross boundaries within and outside the core field of marketing, including "integration of supply and demand management with and across companies, including coordination and collaboration with channel partners and customers, sourcing, procurement, conversion, and logistics" (Mentzer and Gundlach 2010, p. 1). The CSCMP provides the following all-encompassing definition:

> Supply chain management encompasses the planning and management of all activities involved in sourcing and procurement, conversion, and all logistics management activities. Importantly, it also includes coordination and collaboration with channel partners, which can be suppliers, intermediaries, third party service providers, and customers. In essence, supply chain management integrates supply and demand management within and across companies.

In addition, CSCMP also defines the boundaries and relationships involved in SCM. Such boundaries can of course be debated and can be contingency-based (i.e., different in different industries and/or from situation to situation). However, in the interest of capturing the leading SCM association's viewpoint on the boundaries and relationships involved in SCM, their directly quoted statement is set forth. CSCMP states that the boundaries and relationships inherent in SCM are viewed as follows:

> Supply chain management is an integrating function with primary responsibility for linking major business functions and business processes within and across companies into a cohesive and high-performing business model. It includes all of the logistics management activities noted above, as well as manufacturing operations, and it drives coordination of processes and activities with and across marketing, sales, product design, finance, and information technology.

Both the SCM definition and the statement regarding the boundaries and relationships inherent in SCM were found on the CSCMP website on January 1, 2012, at http://cscmp.org/aboutcscmp/definitions.asp. The SCM definition corresponds to the one used by Mentzer and Gundlach (2010) in their introduction to the special issue of the *Journal of the Academy of Marketing Science* on "Exploring the Relationship Between Marketing and SCM."

Customer Relationship Management Processes

Srivastava et al. (1999, p. 172) state that "the change to a market-driven CRM process entails shifting from a modus operandi that views customer relationships as solely means to sell, deliver, and service a product to one that regards them as a means to learn about customer needs and wants and how best to create, satisfy, and sustain them." That statement correlates with their notion that CRM is mostly externally focused and, likewise, correlates with the external emphasis of Day's (1994) "outside-in processes." His external emphasis includes capabilities associated with market sensing, customer linking, channel bonding, and technology monitoring. Srivastava et al.'s (1999, p. 170) external focus includes subprocesses such as "identifying new customers"; "determining the needs of existing and potential new customers"; "learning about product usage and application"; "developing/executing advertising programs"; "developing/executing promotion programs"; "developing/executing service programs"; "developing/executing sales programs"; "acquiring/leveraging information technology/system for customer contact"; "managing customer site visit teams"; and "cross-selling and upselling of product service offerings."

Collectively, it is clear that the combination of Day's (1994) and Srivastava et al.'s (1999) views places a lot more emphasis on the "relationship" aspects in dealing with customers than does the old selling mode. CRM can be an important way to enhance customer loyalty and ultimately the performance of the firm (Hillebrand et al. 2011). But, more importantly, it places an increased focus on the strategic aspects of CRM within the context of the boundary-spanning marketing organization. That is, we assume—based on the external focus suggested by Day (1994) and Srivastava et al. (1999) in this context—CRM capabilities and (marketing) activities are intertwined within the networks that engage the organization (involving multiple or even numerous supply chains) and with the organization's most important (other) processes and activities (e.g., product development). In particular, there is a so-called liability of outsidership (Johanson and Vahlne 2009) of not being inside the appropriate networks, and much of this outsidership can be traced to poor CRM practices (if we assume that the organization has something valuable that the insider network members would want to engage within the context of their products, services, and/or operations). In essence, superior CRM practices may even be able to reduce market uncertainty across the domestic and global marketplace (cf. Johanson and Vahlne 2009).

Complementarity and Combinative Effects

As I stated earlier in this section on customer value-creating processes (i.e., "three core business processes"; Srivastava et al. 1999, p. 169), I believe that both theoretically and practically there is strong potential to develop these processes into "strategic resources" (e.g., Barney 1991; Hult et al. 2003a, 2006) by focusing on elements of complementarity (dependence) and/or the combinative effects (synergy) that can and even should exist among these customer–value-creating processes (cf. Craighead et al. 2009). Literatures on both concepts—complementarity and combinative effects—have developed largely separately, but I believe they can be nicely integrated. The most logical starting point is combinative capabilities, as conceptualized by Kogut and Zander (1992).

Kogut and Zander's (1992) heavily cited research on "combinative capabilities" is anchored in the knowledge of the firm (Grant 1996, 2002). They argue that "what firms do better than markets is the sharing and transfer of the knowledge of individuals and groups within organizations" (Kogut and Zander 1992, p. 383). The logic is that creating new knowledge does not occur independently from the firm's current capabilities. Instead, new knowledge is a function of a firm's combinative capabilities to generate new applications, views, and innovations from existing (but often scattered) knowledge. In that sense, combinative capabilities refer to the "intersection of the capability of the firm to exploit its knowledge and the unexplored potential of the technology" (Kogut and Zander 1992, p. 391). Likewise, the potential of the unique and perhaps idiosyncratic intersections (i.e., combinations) that can be created among the NPD, CRM, and SCM processes (including their many subprocesses) within the boundary-spanning marketing organization can be remarkably important in developing the organization's (sustainable) strategic resources (Barney 1991; Hult and Ketchen 2001; Hult et al. 2002, 2004, 2007b).

Hess and Rothaermel (2011, p. 895) recently discussed the notion of "when are assets complementary" within the context of value chain activities. They addressed this complementarity in a methodological way as "activity combinations," which brings their complementarity idea close to Kogut and Zander (1992). However, the original notion of complementarity is theoretically solid. That is, in its most simplistic form, the logic is as follows. Take the basic formula of $A+B \rightarrow C$. When tested together, both A and B positively affect C. However, if the test entailed $A \rightarrow C$

and B→C in two simplistic regression models and neither A nor B significantly affected C, then we can argue that "complementarity" exists between A and B. Specifically, A and B are significant only if tested jointly on C. This is different from Kogut and Zander's (1992) "combinative capabilities" (or "combinative effects" in my language) in that the Kogut and Zander (1992) theory would require the product of A and B to also be significant (i.e., A + B + A*B →C, where each of A, B, and A*B significantly affects C).

This complementarity and combinative modeling is powerful from a theory standpoint but also logical as it pertains to the customer value-creating processes. For example, marketing organizations that are superior at new product development but cannot support their product development processes with solid CRM and/or SCM processes are at least likely to be less successful in the marketplace (i.e., they are taking advantage of the combinative effects only in a limited way) and may even be achieving no market success due to their lack of good operational CRM and SCM processes (i.e., they lack the complementarity needed among PDM, CRM, and/or SCM processes). This is not to say that marketing organizations should be superior, or even great, at all three core business processes, but they should strive to be great or superior in one of the processes and "neutral" (i.e., average to good) in the other two processes.

Networks

Achrol and Kotler (1999, p. 148) define a network organization as "an independent coalition of task- or skill-specialized economic entities (independent firms or autonomous organizational units) that operates without hierarchical control but is embedded, by dense lateral connections, mutuality, and reciprocity, in a shared value system that defines 'membership' roles and responsibilities." As such, networks consist of units linked together by the fact that they either produce or use complementary or competitive sources (cf. Dickson 1992). Consequently, the network always contains elements of both cooperation and conflict. Achrol and Kotler (1999) distinguish among four types of networks: internal networks, vertical networks, intermarket networks, and opportunity networks (cf. Iacobucci 1996). A boundary-spanning marketing organization adopts one or a subset of these networks based on the adaptability and flexibility required to achieve a competitive advantage (Weick 1976). The connections within each network type involve activity links, actors, and resource ties (Anderson et al. 1994), a conceptualization I used previously in a supply chain setting (Hult 1995).

Internal networks are developed to reduce hierarchy and open marketing organizations to their environments as layered networks and/or internal market networks. Marketing activities are distributed throughout the internal network, with each involved unit being a customer of inputs and marketer of outputs to other units inside and outside the firm. Vertical networks are constructed to maximize the productivity of serially dependent functions by creating partnerships among independent, skill-specialized firms. Marketing activities are specialized in one or a few of the firms in the vertical network to allow this form of network to derive its competitive advantage from a quasi-organizational design. Intermarket networks seek to leverage horizontal synergies across industries. They are held together by a combination of shared resources, strategic decisions, collective action, and social ties. Marketing activities in the intermarket network are similar to those in the vertical network, but unique opportunities exist for marketing in "brokering complex, nontraditional deals among nations, for example, barer, countertrade, and 'third-country' trade" (Achrol and Kotler 1999, p. 156). Opportunity networks are organized around customer needs and market opportunities and are designed to search for the best solution. Marketing activities in the customer opportunity network largely focus on expert knowledge of the dynamics of the marketplace (industrial products) and efficient processing of transactions (customer products).

Overall, marketing activities (or activity links), actors, and resource ties serve as the bonding links within networks of the boundary-spanning marketing organization (cf. Anderson et al. 1994), with each organization adopting a particular network type(s) (internal, vertical, intermarket, opportunity) based on the knowledge, resources, and flexibility needed to achieve a competitive advantage in the marketplace. Each of the three network components—actors, activities, and resources—is dependent on the other two (Håkansson 1989). Specifically, based on Håkansson and Johanson (1984), the dependencies among the three network components are rooted in functional interdependencies, power structure, knowledge structure, and intertemporal dependence.

With respect to the functional interdependence, actors, activities, and resources together form a system where heterogeneous demands are satisfied by heterogenous resources. They are functionally related to each other. Regarding the power structure, based on the control of activities and resources there are important power relations between the actors. The performance of the activities is to some extent organized based on those power relations. Regarding knowledge structures, the design of the activities and the use of the resources are bound together by the knowledge and experience of present and earlier actors. The knowledge of those actors is related to each other. Regarding the intertemporal dependence, the network is a product of its history in terms of all memories, investments in relationships, knowledge, and routines. Changes in the network(s) must be accepted by at least large parts of the network.

Actors in the Network

The actors in the network control activities and resources; individuals, groups of individuals, parts of firms, and groups of firms can be actors (Håkansson and Johanson 1984; Håkansson and Östberg 1975). This means that a functional department within the organization can assume the position of one individual actor when dealing with both inter- and intra-network members (Håkansson 1989). Thus, in the boundary-spanning marketing organization network, actors operate at several organizational levels. Hence, actors at lower levels can be part of actors at higher levels (i.e., a functional department can assume the position of one single actor although it consists of actors at different hierarchical levels). Independent of the level, actors have five basic characteristics (Håkansson and Johanson 1984). First, they perform and control the activities within the network(s), meaning that they determine, alone or jointly, which activities to perform, how these activities are to be performed, and which resources are to be used when performing the activities. Second, through exchange processes actors develop relationships with each other, with each actor being embedded in a web of relationships which indirectly or directly give the actor access to other actors' resources (Iacobucci and Hopkins 1992). The interaction process, the participants themselves, the environment, and the atmosphere affect the development of actor-specific relationships in network(s) (Håkansson 1987, 1992). Third, actors base their activities on direct (i.e., ownership) or indirect control over resources. Indirect control is relatively intangible but critically important in the network; it is generally based on relationships with other actors and the associated dependence relationships with those actors (e.g., Dant and Schul 1992; Gaski 1984; Heide and John 1988; Keith et al. 1990). Fourth, actors are goal-oriented, with the general goal of increasing their control over the network (power and influence within the structural boundary-spanning organizational system, assuming that control is a means to achieve other goals). Fifth, actors possess certain knowledge about activities, resources, and other actors in the network(s). Typically, the knowledge of closer parts of the network is greater than the knowledge of more distant parts.

Activity Links in the Network

An activity occurs when one or several actors combine, develop, exchange, or create resources by utilizing other resources (cf. Hunt 2000). Activities performed within a unit are typically called "production activities," and activities performed between units are typically called "exchange activities" within the network perspective (e.g., Håkansson 1989). Both sets of activities within network(s) are clearly important, but the exchange activities take on a particularly important role given the scope of the boundary-spanning marketing organization. The dependencies among the production activities, exchange activities, and across the production and exchange activities are critically important in the context of the larger depiction of the boundary-spanning marketing organization. Specifically, a change in one relation can often effect other network relations, and to varied degrees a small change in one relation in some cases ultimately leads to a significant effect on the network in other places far removed from that one small change (cf. "bullwhip effect" in SCM). The need for coordination to avoid this bullwhip effect in the network is determined by the dependence relationships between activities. Several types of dependencies generally coexist in the network(s). First, a sequential dependency refers to a situation in which some activities must be carried out before others. Second, a shared dependency exists in the system when two or more activities are mutually dependent on each other because they are linked together by a common entity. Importantly, the inter-unit exchange activities are important to bridge the gaps between production activities within units and to channel and handle a variety of conflicting forces in the network. Within this network context, two categories of activities exist: transformation and transfer (Håkansson 1987). Transformation activities are always carried out within the control of one of the actors. They are characterized by one resource being improved by the use of other resources. Transfer activities link transformation activities, forming chains of activities and creating relationships with other actors.

Resource Ties in the Network

The resource ties represent a necessary condition for all intra-unit activities (Håkansson 1989; Pfeffer and Salancik 1978; Thompson 1967). In the case of the individual units within network(s), five types of resources can be identified (Håkansson 1989, 1992; Waluszewski 1989), each related to some parts of the corporate environment: input goods, financial capital, technology, personnel, and marketing (cf. Barney 1991; Wernerfelt 1984). In the context of these five resources, the underlying foundation for network(s) is the assumption that the network resources are heterogeneous. For example, the performance of one employee depends, to some degree, on those actors with whom they cooperate. As such, this means that as an independent resource within the systematic structure, Resource A is not a constant. Instead, Resource A is affected by the cooperation of others. For such combinations to be effective, actors within the system have to learn to know different actors and/or resources available, and thus to discover the appropriate combinations. Traditionally, an organization thrived on the notion that it was better at dealing with the creation of "appropriate combinations" of resources, actors, and activity links than was the external market. Likewise, the expectation is that the boundary-spanning marketing organization is better at the creation of "appropriate combinations" of resources, actors, and activity links than are those organizations that are not a part of the network (e.g., Johanson and Vahlne 2009, 2011).

Stakeholders

Freeman (1984, p. 46) defines stakeholders as "any group or individual who can affect or is affected by the achievement of the organization's objectives." Stakeholders are categorized into two core groups: primary and secondary (Clarkson 1995; Hult et al. 2011). Primary stakeholders are those on whom the marketing organization depends for its survival (i.e., shareholders, employees, customers, suppliers, regulators, and local communities) (e.g., Hult et al. 2011). Secondary stakeholders (e.g., special interest groups, competitors, trade associations, mass media, and social media) do not have a strong or direct tie to the marketing organization, cannot exercise any legal authority over the organization, and are not vital for its survival (e.g., Eesley and Lenox 2006; Hult et al. 2011). This also means that the influence of the primary stakeholders is weighted more heavily in developing a marketing organization's strategies (cf. Ferrell et al. 2010) to achieve superior performance (cf. Hult 2011a; Maignan et al. 1999).

At a coarse-grained level, resource dependence theory (Pfeffer and Salancik 1978) provides the rationale to designate shareholders, employees, customers, suppliers, regulators, and local communities as primary stakeholders. Accordingly, an organization is dependent on "environmental actors" (i.e., stakeholders) who control resources that are critical for its continued survival. For example, the organization depends on customers for sales revenues, employees for human capital, suppliers for raw materials and other inputs (Porter 2008), shareholders for capital investment (Day and Fahey 1988), communities for natural resources (Porter and Kramer 2006), and regulators for access to markets (Birnbaum 1985).

At a fine-grained level, stakeholders can be identified by their possession of at least one of three attributes: power, legitimacy, and urgency (Mitchell et al. 1997). In this context, power is the extent to which an actor can impose his or her will through coercive, utilitarian, or normative means. Legitimacy is defined as "a generalized perception or assumption that the actions of an entity are desirable, proper, or appropriate within some socially constructed system of norms, values, beliefs, and definitions" (Suchman 1995, p. 574). Urgency is the degree to which an actor's demands require immediate attention based on time sensitivity (extent to which a delay is unacceptable to the stakeholder) and criticality (importance of the demands to the stakeholder). Given these restrictions, stakeholder theory views the marketing organization as "an organizational entity through which numerous and diverse participants accomplish multiple, and not always entirely congruent, purposes" (Donaldson and Preston 1995, p. 70). Overall, the relative importance of the primary (and secondary) stakeholders in the boundary-spanning marketing organization is directly dependent on the stakeholders' power, legitimacy, and urgency weighted relative to the criticality of the resources controlled by the respective stakeholder. Hult et al. (2011) provide a comprehensive review of 58 marketing articles on stakeholders and then summarize the conceptual aspects of stakeholders. Using Hult et al. (2011), with an encouragement to refer to their work for more in-depth coverage of stakeholders, I briefly summarize the main aspects of primary and secondary stakeholders in the following two paragraphs.

Primary Stakeholders

Based on Hult et al. (2011), primary stakeholders include customers, employees, suppliers, shareholders, regulators, and local communities. First, customers, as an important stakeholder group, have been tackled in incredible depth in the marketing literature; much of the strategic and consumer-based marketing literatures center on customers, given their centrality in the scope of what marketing entails. Second, employees are often a major source of a firm's success. In fact, employees are instrumental in building customer commitment to the organization, in increasing customers' willingness to pay, and in improving the level of customer satisfaction. Third, a firm's relationships with its suppliers can be instrumental to the firm's ability to achieve superior performance. A well-performing relationship exists when both the supplier and the firm are satisfied with the effectiveness and efficiency of the relationship. Fourth, firms have an important commitment and obligation to shareholders; that is, to maximize their wealth. Shareholders invest in a firm with the expectation that the firm will generate better returns than they could otherwise get. Fifth, regulators are important stakeholders that can exert political and economic restrictions (e.g., regulations, laws) on the firm. Constraints imposed on firms by regulators can have an impact on a variety of activities including, for example, the design of products. Sixth, community stakeholders include nongovernmental organizations and communities formed because of their geography (i.e., proximity) to the firm's operations (e.g., production, sales, and supply chain activities).

Secondary Stakeholders

Based on Hult et al. (2011), secondary stakeholders include special interest groups, competitors, trade associations, mass media, and social media. First, a special interest group is a community with an interest in advancing a particular area of knowledge, topic focus, and/or set of activities. Second, competitors are, within the context of the boundary-spanning marketing organization, both those organizations that are within the network and compete in the same product or service category and those organizations that are not a part of the network pertaining to a specific organization (labeled "outsidership" by Johanson and Vahlne 2009). That actually means that the network has a set of "softer" competitors inside the network ("insidership" by Johanson and Vahlne 2009) and a more concrete set of "harder" competitors outside the network ("outsidership" by Johanson and Vahlne 2009). Third, a trade association is an organization founded and funded by other organizations (or even individuals) that typically operates in a specific industry (although some trade associations are also topic based and span industries). Fourth, mass media refers generally to all media technologies which are designed to reach a large audience via some form of mass communication. Fifth, social media, clearly related to mass media but important enough to distinguish it from mass media in this context (e.g., Hult et al. 2011), refers to web-based and mobile technologies that generally turn communication into an interactive system or dialogue involving their participants (although of course an actor can passively take part as well).

Chapter 3
Organization Theories Can Inform Research on the Marketing Organization

To advance research, the theoretical integration of marketing activities, customer value-creating processes, networks, and stakeholders in the boundary-spanning marketing organization can be informed by a number of organization theories (cf. Ketchen and Hult 2007a, b, 2011; Wind 2009). Thirty-one theories appear particularly applicable to inform work on the marketing organization as conceptualized within the confines of MOR theory (a listing of the 31 organization theories can be found in Table 1.2). These 31 theories have emerged as potentially insightful for studying marketing organizations (cf. Workman et al. 1998) and strategic marketing phenomena (cf. Varadarajan 2010). At the outset, it is important to realize that these 31 organization theories have different arguments, units of analysis, assumptions, antecedents, and/or consequences. It is also important to note that the 31 theories can be used within organizational settings, although an argument can be made that some of them are not necessarily "organization theories" by their origin. Importantly, while a complete integration of any pair of theories is difficult, an integration of 31 theories is impossible. Instead, what I intend to accomplish is to draw out the most applicable aspects of each of the 31 organization theories within the context of the boundary-spanning marketing organization. The idea is that each theory has a unique ability to explain and predict certain aspects of the boundary-spanning marketing organization which cannot be as effectively or efficiently done by another theory.

I selected these 31 theories based on their current use in organization-focused research coupled with their significant application potential for the study of marketing organizations. Obviously other organization and non-organization theories are applicable to marketing organizations. Their omission in this SpringerBrief is by no means an indication that they are not or could not be valuable in explaining and predicting certain cultural, structural, and/or behavioral aspects of marketing organizations. Equally important, while 31 organization theories are used in the SpringerBrief, each is not necessarily equally valid, insightful, and accepted in the marketing and organization literatures and, as such, some theories are used more heavily in the development than others.

G.T.M. Hult, *Boundary-Spanning Marketing Organization: A Theory and Insights from 31 Organization Theories*, SpringerBriefs in Business 20,
DOI 10.1007/978-1-4614-3819-9_3,

For the following discussion, the theories are grouped based on similarity and applicability for the boundary-spanning marketing organization (i.e., strategic marketing resources, marketing leadership and decision-making, network alliances and collaborations, and domestic and global marketplaces). Table 3.1 summarizes in which cluster each organization theory belongs as it pertains to this research. The focus of the clustered review of the organization theories is on the integration of existing organization theory thoughts as opposed to the interpretation of those thoughts. The intended value of such an approach is to provide a "toolkit" to

Table 3.1 A clustered listing of the 31 organization theories

Strategic marketing resources
Adjustment-cost theory of the firm
Competence-based theory
Knowledge-based view of the firm
Resource-advantage theory
Resource-based view of the firm
Service-dominant logic
Theory of the growth of the firm
Marketing leadership and decision-making
Agency theory
Bounded rationality theory
Game theory
Prospect theory
Real options theory
Strategic choice theory
Theory of competitive rationality
Upper echelons theory
Network alliances and collaborations
Behavioral theory of the firm
Information economics theory
Network theory
Resource dependence theory
Signaling theory
Social capital theory
Theory of multimarket competition
Transaction cost economics
Domestic and global marketplace
Contingency theory
Eclectic theory of international production
Industrial organization
Institutional theory
Organizational ecology
Stakeholder theory
Systems theory
Theory of the multinational enterprise

The organization theories are clustered in the groupings used in this research. Clearly, each theory goes well beyond the scope aligned with each cluster. The clusters are simply the structure placed on the theories within the context of this research marketing researchers working in the areas covered in MOR theory (cf. Connelly et al. 2010; Ketchen and Hult 2007a, b, 2011).

In Table 3.2, each theory is summarized in terms of its original and marketing scopes as well as the main marketing insights that can be derived from its use within MOR theory. This summary table is meant to serve as a quick overview of each theory, with direct reference to their original sources and with the basic aspects of each theory explained. In essence, Table 3.2 is the Cliff Notes version of the 31 organization theories but with thoughtful marketing scopes and marketing insights that can set the tone for future research on the boundary-spanning marketing organization, marketing strategy, and perhaps the field of marketing in general.

Strategic Marketing Resources

Seven of the organization theories in Table 3.2 have an intellectual cluster centered on "strategic marketing resources" as they apply to a boundary-spanning marketing organization (i.e., adjustment-cost theory of the firm, competence-based theory, knowledge-based view (KBV) of the firm, resource-advantage theory, resource-based view of the firm (RBV), service-dominant logic, and theory of the growth of the firm). As such, developing, nurturing, and maintaining an advantage in the marketplace is directly tied to strategic (marketing) resources for a marketing organization based on the central elements of the seven "resource theories." Albeit applied somewhat differently in each theory, resources permeate the fabric of each and serve as a focal point for integration and knowledge insights for MOR theory.

- *Theory of the growth of the firm*: Originally focusing on industrial firms, this theory defines the economic function as a collection of resources bound together in an administrative framework. Importantly, it is never the resources that the boundary-spanning marketing organization possesses that serve as inputs in the production process but only the services that the organization's resources can render.
- *RBV*: Marketing activities tie resources with advantage and performance in the boundary-spanning marketing organization. The RBV envisions the organization as a collection of strategic resources which are heterogeneously distributed across firms.
- *Resource-advantage theory*: A disequilibrium-seeking process can increase resources, even if certain resources are used up. The basis for a sustainable competitive advantage resides in the boundary-spanning marketing organization's resources and in how it structures, bundles, and leverages those resources.
- *Competence-based theory*: This theory addresses what the firm can do particularly well in relation to its competition. The focus is on capabilities that make the whole boundary-spanning marketing organization more productive than the sum of its internal and external units.
- *KBV of the firm*: With a focus on "strategic knowledge," the firm is portrayed as an institution for integrating knowledge. The implication is that marketing

Table 3.2 The 31 organization theories: original scope, marketing scope, and marketing insights

Theory	Original scope	Marketing scope	Marketing insights
Adjustment-cost theory of the firm	The adjustment-cost theory of the firm (Wernerfelt 1997) "examines ongoing trading relationships and asks by which process the parties should adjust the relationship by accommodating changes" (Wernerfelt 2005, p. 17)	The adjustment-cost theory of the firm examines ongoing marketing relationships and asks by which process the supply chain should adjust the relationship by accommodating changes in individual marketing organizations and their marketing strategies	The marketing organization's use of strategic marketing resources is correlated with a need for frequent and diverse marketing adaptations. A horizontal expansion should govern the marketing organization's transfer of any excess strategic marketing resource capacity if it entails frequent and diverse marketing adaptations If the industry places a premium on flexibility in the marketing organization's interactions with its supply chains, the adjustment-cost theory suggests that the marketing organization should expand its vertical scope by bringing in parts of the supply chain(s)
Agency theory	Agency theory explains firm governance by delineating firm owners as principals that hire agents (managers) to carry out the business of operating the organization (Jensen and Meckling 1976)	Agency theory explains the governance of marketing organizations by delineating firm owners as principals that hire agents (marketing managers) to carry out the business of operating the marketing organization (Jensen and Meckling 1976)	A central element of agency theory is the so-called agency problem; it arises when the interests of the marketing manager and owner(s) of the firm diverge. Due to information asymmetry between marketing managers and owner(s), the possibility exists that the marketing managers will act opportunistically, in their own interests, rather than those of the owners "Because cross-cultural differences magnify the problems of uncertainty, asymmetric information, and monitoring, efficient agency relationships can be even more difficult to achieve in multinational markets than in domestic markets" (Bergen et al. 1992, p. 18)

Behavioral theory of the firm	The behavioral theory of the firm holds that organizations should be viewed as consisting of a number of coalitions and the role of management is to achieve resolution of conflict and uncertainty avoidance within the confines of bounded rationality (Cyert and March 1963/1992)	The behavioral theory of the firm suggest that marketing organizations should be viewed as consisting of a number of marketing coalitions and the role of marketing management is to achieve resolution of conflict and uncertainty avoidance within the confines of bounded rationality (Cyert and March 1963/1992)	The marketing organization operates within the confines of "imperfect environmental matching, the observation that the rules, forms, and practices used by economic [marketing] actors are not uniquely determined by the demands of the environmental setting in which they arise" (Cyert and March 1963/1992, p. 215) The marketing organization operates within the confines of "unresolved conflict, the assumption that economic [marketing] organizations involve multiple [marketing] actors with conflicting interests not entirely resolved by employment contracts" (Cyert and March 1963/1992, p. 215)
Bounded rationality theory	Bounded rationality (a.k.a. theory of bounded rationality) recognizes that it is not possible to understand and analyze all information that is potentially relevant in making firm choices; to cope with their complexity, firms develop techniques, habits, and operating procedures to facilitate decision-making (Simon 1945, 1957)	Bounded rationality recognizes that it is not possible to understand and analyze all market and marketing information that is potentially relevant in making choices for the marketing organization and its marketing strategy; to cope with the complexity in which the firm operates, including its marketplace, it develops marketing techniques, habits, and operating procedures to facilitate decision-making	The rationality of marketing managers is limited by the information they have and/or can obtain, the cognitive limitations of their minds and frame of reference, and the time constraint in which they have to make decisions to develop the marketing organization and/or its marketing strategy Marketing managers are "intendedly rational, but only boundedly so" (Simon 1945/1997, p. 88), which means that rational behavior and limits of rationality are the basic premises for marketing managers in developing marketing organizations and forming marketing strategy

(continued)

Table 3.2 (continued)

Theory	Original scope	Marketing scope	Marketing insights
Competence-based theory	Competence-based theory is an "internal factors theory of business strategy" (Hunt 2000, p. 80) which traces to Selznick's (1957) work on "distinctive competence." It was used by Andrews (1971) to refer to what the firm could do particularly well in relation to its competition	Competence-based theory lends itself uniquely to the study of the marketing organization in that it focuses its sole attention on the distinctive competencies that make the marketing organization thrive in a competitive environment	"It is organizational [marketing] capabilities that make the whole firm more productive than the sum of its operating units" (Chandler 1990, p. 15), such as the marketing organization or marketing function; thus, an effective organization is dependent on marketing capabilities permeating throughout the fabric of the firm, filtering through the marketing organization The "essence of [marketing] strategy lies in creating tomorrow's competitive advantages faster than competitors mimic the ones you possess today," which implies that marketing organizations should invest in core competencies given that "an organization's capacity to improve existing skills and learn new ones is the most defensible competitive advantage of all" (Hamel and Prahalad 1989, p. 69)
Contingency theory	Contingency theory is an outgrowth of systems design and "is guided by the general orienting hypothesis that organizations whose internal features best match the demands of their environments will achieve the best adaptation… the best way to organize depends on the nature of the environment to which the organization relates" (Scott 2005, p. 89)	Based on Gailbraith (1973), contingency theory suggests that (1) there is no one best way to organize a marketing organization and (2) each way of organizing a marketing organization is not equally effective	Different subunits within a marketing organization may face different market demands. To tackle these various market conditions, marketing organizations need to create specialized subunits with differing structural features—for example, different levels of formalization, planning time horizon With increased variation in the market conditions faced by the marketing organization, its structure needs to be more differentiated to face all potential challenges in the marketplace

Eclectic theory of international production	The eclectic theory of international production (Dunning 1980) provides a three-tiered framework for a firm to use in determining if it is beneficial to pursue a foreign direct investment (FDI). It centers on advantages in the areas of ownership (production or firm specific advantages such as comparative advantage), location-specific advantages, and market internalization (i.e., it may be better for the firm itself to exploit an international opportunity than through an agreement with a foreign firm; Buckley and Casson 1976)	The eclectic theory centers on advantages in production for the marketing organization such as comparative advantage, location-specific advantages of being in the right place at the right time internationally, and market internalization (e.g., home country produced products and services vs. offshoring production vs. outsourcing). As such, Dunning's OLI theory is not a theory of the firm per se; instead it is a theory of a firm's FDI	The marketing organization's advantage is often intangible and can be transferred within the multinational corporation at a low cost (e.g., technology, brand name, economies of scale). This market and/or marketing advantage gives rise to greater revenues and/or lower costs that may offset the costs of operating at a distance in an international location The marketing organization must use some foreign factors in connection with its home country–specific advantages in order to earn full rents. The location advantages of different countries are keys in determining which country or countries will become host countries for the multinational corporation The multinational corporation has a number of choices of entry mode into international markets, beginning with the market (arm's length transactions) and spanning to the hierarchy (wholly-owned subsidiary). The marketing organization, in this context, selects internalization when the market does not exist or when it functions poorly

(continued)

Table 3.2 (continued)

Theory	Original scope	Marketing scope	Marketing insights
Game theory	Game theory is rooted in applied mathematics but has been used in a variety of fields, including organizational theory, to capture behavior in strategic situations; the focus in such scenarios has been on an individual's success in making strategic choices relative to other players in the organization and/or marketplace with a goal of finding the equilibrium in the "game" itself, where each player has adopted a strategy that is unlikely to change (Neumann and Morgenstern 1944)	Game theory is a collection of mathematical models that can be formulated to study market and marketing decision-making in situations involving conflict and cooperation (e.g., within a marketing organization or in the marketplace), with the end goal of developing optimal solutions or stable marketing outcomes when the involved players (e.g., marketing decisionmakers) have conflicting marketing objectives in mind (cf. Lucas 1972)	Game theory can be used in the marketing organization to develop marketing strategy through gaining a better theoretical understanding of decision-making choices and potential outcomes in potential give-and-take and/or competitive market situations. The outcomes of possible scenarios can be depicted in game matrices, with optimal solutions being determined based on a variety of different assumptions Game theory can help indicate the outcomes of different strategic choices for rational marketing organizations in dynamic situations. Due to limitations associated with the theory (e.g., usually less than optimal information available, potential irrational behavioral actions by the players), game theory should not necessarily be expected to result in precise solutions to marketing organization or marketing strategy problems. To overcome such limitations, subjective-probability judgments or risk assessment by decision makers can be employed to reduce uncertainty (di Benedetto 1987)

Industrial organization	Industrial organization (a.k.a. industrial organization economics) is rooted in economics and focuses on the strategic behavior of firms, the structure of markets, and their interactions (Bain 1956, 1959; Chamberlin 1933; Mason 1939), ultimately affecting the performance of firms (Schmalensee 1985)	Industrial organization focuses on the strategic marketing behavior of marketing organizations, the structure of the marketplace in which they operate, and the interactions among marketing strategy and market structure. Synergy between marketing strategy and the market structure serve as the essential scope to leverage market performance	In line with the structure-conduct-performance approach, the market success of an industry in developing products and/or services for customers depends on the collective actions of the firms in the industry. The market actions of the firms depend on the actors who determine the competitiveness of the market. Tied to the marketing organization, the competitiveness of the market is a function of innovations, technology, and marketing strategy Following classical logic, marketing organizations within an industry are identical regarding the market resources they control. However, should resource heterogeneity develop, it will likely be temporary, given that market resources are highly mobile. As such, homogeneity of marketing strategies among organizations competing in the same industry exists since, for example, marketing actions taken by a firm are easily observable and duplicated by other firms

(continued)

Table 3.2 (continued)

Theory	Original scope	Marketing scope	Marketing insights
Information economics theory	Information economics (a.k.a. economics of information) is a branch of microeconomic theory focused on how information affects economic decisions of a firm; a key element is that information has economic value (Akerlof 1970; Spence 1974; Stiglitz 1961)	Information economics focuses on how information generation and dissemination affect resource allocation and decisions of a marketing organization; a key element is that information has economic value in the sense of the value to understanding the market, developing products/services to meet the needs of the market, and then responding accordingly to market needs (cf. market orientation)	Two critical aspects of information economics theory, rooted in the notion of information asymmetry, are "signaling" (see also signaling theory in this table) and "screening." Both of these elements provide insights for marketing Related to signaling in the context of information economics: In a situation of information asymmetry, marketing organizations can signal to the marketplace what type of organization they are (e.g., an organization dedicated to sustainability practices), thus transferring information to the organization's stakeholders (most notably its customers in the marketplace) and resolving the information asymmetry Related to screening: The underinformed party (e.g., customers) can induce the other party (e.g., marketing organization) to reveal more information about its products, services, strategy, or organization

Institutional theory	"Institutional theory attends to the deeper and more resilient aspects of social structure … it considers the processes by which structures, including schemas, rules, norms, and routines, become established as authoritative guidelines for social behavior … it inquiries into how these elements are created, diffused, adopted, and adapted over space and time; and how they fall into decline and disuse" (Scott 2005, p. 461)	Institutional theory focuses on the marketplace (environmental) factors that are experienced by a marketing organization, such as industry or societal norms, regulations, and requirements that an organization must conform to in order to receive legitimacy and marketplace support Institutional theory depends on the social constructs, informal and formal marketing exchanges to help define the structure and processes of an organization	To attain legitimacy, a marketing organization tends to be isomorphic to other organizations in its market environment, with organizations resembling each other and behaving similarly over time (e.g., Dacin 1997). As such, the way a particular marketing organization interacts with and treats its customers influences other organizations' interactions with their customers (cf. Webb et al. 2011) Organizations' marketing strategies can converge via three mechanisms—coercive, mimetic, and normative (DiMaggio and Powell 1983). Coercive isomorphism is driven by market legitimacy, where organizations will imitate others that they are dependent on in order to attain legitimacy. Mimetic isomorphism will arise under conditions of market uncertainty, whereby organizations will mimic others in their field, especially those they regard as more successful or those with whom they have boundary-spanning ties. Normative isomorphism stems from the propagation of norms through social networks, where members of an organization will learn which marketing practices are considered appropriate within the field

(continued)

Table 3.2 (continued)

Theory	Original scope	Marketing scope	Marketing insights
Knowledge-based view of the firm	"The emerging knowledge-based view of the firm is not a theory of the firm in any formal sense" (Grant 2002, p. 135). However, "given the assumptions about the characteristics of knowledge and the knowledge requirements of production, the firm is conceptualized as an institution for integrating knowledge" (Grant 1996, p. 109)	Given the assumptions about the characteristics of market and marketing knowledge and the knowledge requirements of developing and implementing marketing strategy, the marketing organization is conceptualized as an institution for integrating market and marketing knowledge	There is an implicit assumption that there is value and that production gains can be realized by having marketing professionals specializing in knowledge acquisition and organizational memory storage (cf. Hanvanich et al. 2006). Development of marketing strategy and the accompanying product and service assortment requires the input and coordination of a wide range of specialized market and marketing knowledge If the primary productive resource of the marketing organization is market and/or marketing knowledge, and if knowledge resides in individual marketing professionals, then it is the marketing professionals (at all levels of hierarchy) who own the bulk of the marketing organization's resources (cf. Hult 2003)
Network theory	Network theory (a.k.a. social network theory, as applied to organizations) involves the creation of a blend of strong and weak ties between nodes that match the firm's needs in order to maximize the firm's performance. Network theory describes, explains, and predicts relations among linked entities (e.g., Granovetter 1973; Thorelli 1986)	Network theory views marketing relationships as consisting of actors (i.e., nodes), resource ties, and activity links (Håkansson 1989). Actors control the resources and perform the activities. Activities link resources to each other; an activity occurs when one or several actors combines, develops, exchanges, or creates resources by using other resources. Resources, in the network context, include input goods, financial capital, technology, personnel, and marketing	Strong and weak ties are often formed on a case-by-case basis rather than strategically across marketing organizations in a network Often a blend of strong and weak ties that matches the firm's marketing needs should be created proactively in order to maximize performance for each marketing organization within the network Actors (e.g., marketing organizations, marketing professionals), activity links (e.g., forming supply chains involving multiple actors), and resource ties (e.g., joint market orientation efforts among marketing organizations) bind the network together

Organizational ecology	Organizational ecology (a.k.a. organizational demography, population ecology of organizations) focuses on understanding the environmental conditions under which organizations emerge, grow, and die (Hannan and Freeman 1977)	Organizational ecology focuses on understanding the environmental conditions (e.g., market turbulence, technological turbulence, competitive intensity) under which marketing organizations emerge, grow and change, and die	New marketing organizations and new organizational forms (e.g., vertically and/or horizontally integrated organizations) will arise that are well suited to contemporary marketing strategy Marketing organizations that do not adapt their culture, processes, and activities to become appropriately market oriented may be selected out of the population (i.e., marketplace)
Prospect theory	Prospect theory (a.k.a. cumulative prospect theory, as a revised version of the original prospect theory) describes how organizations (or people) make choices between alternatives that involve degrees of risk; the theory focuses on how organizations (or people) evaluate potential losses or gains (Kahneman and Tversky 1979)	Prospect theory describes how marketing organizations make choices between marketing strategy alternatives that involve degrees of marketplace risk, with the evaluation being on the marketplace gains or potential losses that may be incurred by the organization	Prospect theory leaves it up to the marketing manager to subjectively frame a marketing outcome or transaction in their mind. Such framing affects the marketing utility which can be expected to be obtained by the marketing organization. The issue of "framing," within the confines of prospect theory, is generally considered to be inconsistent with economic rationality but is important for the subjective rationale within the notion of "marketing rationality" The marketing utility is reference based, in contrast with the additive economic utility functions which serve as a foundation for neo-classical economics. As such, marketing organizations should consider not only the marketing value they receive but also the marketing value received by other marketing organizations in their network

(continued)

Table 3.2 (continued)

Theory	Original scope	Marketing scope	Marketing insights
Real options theory	Rooted in techniques developed for valuing financial options (Trigeorgis 1996), real options theory (a.k.a. real options analysis) focuses on risk uncertainty and revolves around creating and then exercising or not exercising certain options (Myers 1977)	Real options theory focuses on market and marketing investments in real marketing assets, as opposed to financial assets, which affords the organization the right (but not the obligation) to undertake specific marketing actions in the future	Marketing managers should look beyond the net present value of a marketing investment and consider the value of the options offered by such an investment (cf. Homburg et al. 2010a). In this context, a real option has as its underlying marketing asset the total value of the marketing project, with the cost being the investment required to obtain the asset and the time to maturity being reflected in the period in which the marketing manager can defer the investment before it expires Exogenous uncertainty in the marketplace lies beyond the reach of marketing managers' control, although it may be reduced as market events unfold (e.g., product development, research and development activities, target market assessment, market segmentation analysis). A prime example is international marketing, as the international marketplace is often seen as having high levels of uncertainty and heterogeneous opportunities being presented across varied countries
Resource-advantage theory	Resource-advantage theory (a.k.a. "the comparative advantage theory of competition"; Hunt and Morgan 1995; "a general theory of competition"; Hunt 2000) suggests that the basis for a sustainable competitive advantage resides in an organization's resources and in how it structures, bundles, and leverages those resources (Hunt and Morgan 1995)	The original scope of R-A theory was developed in a marketing context. Given its marketing foundation, the resource-advantage theory envisions the marketing organization as a bundle of marketing resources that is rooted in a disequilibrium-seeking process embedded in a marketplace of less than perfect competition	Strategic marketing practices and operations can provide a competitive advantage for all marketing organizations in the marketplace Resource-advantage theory stresses that marketing productivity and economic growth are furthered through both the efficient allocation of scarce tangible marketing resources and the creation of new intangible and tangible marketing resources

Resource-based view of the firm	The resource-based view of the firm (Wernerfelt 1984) envisions the firm as a collection of strategic resources which are heterogeneously distributed across firms (Barney 1991) to achieve a sustainable competitive advantage	The resource-based view of the firm envisions the marketing organization as a bundle of strategic marketing resources which are heterogeneously distributed across marketing organizations and are rooted in an equilibrium-seeking process embedded in a marketplace of perfect competition	The RBV (Wernerfelt 1984) "is based on the premise that firms differ, even within an industry. The differences occur in the firms' resources, and the main theory is that a firm's strategy should depend on its resources—if a firm is good at something, the firm should try to use it" (Wernerfelt 2005, p. 17) Strategic marketing resources have only potential value, with the value ultimately being realized (or not) via organizational actions and behaviors; realizing the potential value also requires alignment with other important marketing organization and/or marketing strategy elements (cf. Ketchen et al. 2007)
Resource dependence theory	Resource dependence theory describes the sources and consequences of power of organizations embedded in networks of interdependencies and social networks that revolve around the control of and dependence on vital external resources in the environment (Pfeffer and Salancik 1978)	Resource dependence theory suggests that the sources and consequences of power that marketing organizations have in the marketplace depend on their industry-specific marketing networks and alignment with supply chain partners that revolve around the control and dependence on strategic marketing resources created by interaction with the external environment	A marketing organization's ability to implement marketing strategy and operational marketing practices may be constrained when they are dependent on other organizations within their supply chains and industrial networks The external environment contains limited marketing resources, so marketing organizations must learn to hold back at times in developing marketing strategy that is resource dependent and trust each other if they are going to coexist successfully over time

(continued)

Table 3.2 (continued)

Theory	Original scope	Marketing scope	Marketing insights
Service-dominant logic	Service-dominant logic "implies that the goal is to customize offerings, to recognize that the consumer is always a coproducer, and to strive to maximize consumer involvement in the customization to better fit his or her needs" (Vargo and Lusch 2004, p. 12). In S-D logic, "*service* is defined as the application of specialized competences (operant resources—knowledge skills), through deeds, processes, and performances for the benefit of another entity or the entity itself" (Vargo and Lusch 2008, p. 2)	The original scope of S-D logic was developed within a marketing context. Given its marketing foundation, "a service-centered view identifies operant [marketing] resources, especially higher-order, core [marketing] competences, as the key to obtaining competitive advantage" for a marketing organization (Vargo and Lusch 2004, p. 12)	Vargo and Lusch (2008, p. 29) provide a number of "marketing theory implications of service" and S-D logic, as do the "foundational premises" offered by Vargo and Lusch (2004, 2008) and the "dialog" in Lusch and Vargo (2006). Their point on knowledge being the fundamental source of competitive advantage has strong and direct implications for the theory of the marketing organization "The use of knowledge as the basis for competitive advantage can be extended to the entire 'supply chain,' or service-provision chain … we argue that the primary flow [in the supply chain] is information; *service* is the provision of the information to (or use of the information for) a consumer who desires it, with or without an accompanying appliance" (Vargo and Lusch 2004, p. 9) "The move toward a service-dominant logic is grounded in an increased focus on operant resources and specifically process management" (Vargo and Lusch 2004, p. 10). This process focus overlaps the view of the "marketing process organization" by Moorman and Rust (1999) and the business process focus by Srivastava et al. (1999)

Signaling theory	Signaling theory involves one firm (the agent) conveying some meaningful information about itself and/or its products and services to another party (the principal) (Spence 1973)	Signaling theory involves one marketing organization conveying some meaningful market, product, or service information to customers and/or another party in their marketplace	It is difficult for consumers to know which marketing organizations are genuinely committed to business practices with which they associate and with whom they desire to buy products. In this context, some marketing organizations use costly marketing initiatives to "signal" the type of organization they are and the products that they sell to reduce information asymmetry Marketing organizations may go out of their way to "signal" a particular issue, product, or service feature to the market as a form of market positioning and even market segmentation
Social capital theory	Social capital theory's central premise is that networks of relationships constitute a valuable resource for the conduct of social affairs (Nahapiet and Ghoshal 1998, p. 242), providing their members with "the collectivity-owned capital, a 'credential' which entitles them to credit, in the various senses of the word" (Bourdieu 1986, p. 249)	Social capital theory recognizes that marketing organizations and the marketplace are composed of people (e.g., customers, salespeople) and that interpersonal skills and relationships among these people (such as the "credits" and trust they build with each other) shape a marketing organization's activities and outcomes	A mixture of shared and organization-level goals, values, and experiences drive marketing strategy-making, which leads to superior success for a marketing organization in the marketplace Sensemaking among individuals in and between marketing organizations is a key to trust building in supply chains and market networks

(continued)

Table 3.2 (continued)

Theory	Original scope	Marketing scope	Marketing insights
Stakeholder theory	Stakeholder theory addresses morals and values in managing a firm that has to deal with a multitude of constituent groups other than shareholders (Freeman 1984); it views the firm as "an organizational entity through which numerous and diverse participants accomplish multiple, and not always entirely congruent, purposes" (Donaldson and Preston 1995, p. 70)	Stakeholder theory focuses the marketing organization's efforts on developing and nurturing exchanges with a multitude of constituent groups other than customers and shareholders. As such, the stakeholder approach seeks to broaden a marketing manager's vision of his/her responsibilities beyond being customer and profit oriented (cf. Mitchell et al. 1997)	Managing primary stakeholder relationships (i.e., customers, employees, suppliers, shareholders, communities, and regulators) is essential for the marketing organization because not doing so can be detrimental to the achievement of marketing objectives Managing secondary stakeholder relationships (e.g., media, special interest groups) may also be critical as a marketing communications (e.g., advertising, public relations) plan for the marketing organization to succeed in the marketplace
Strategic choice theory	Strategic choice theory contends that managers' decisions play a tremendous role in a firm's success or failure, with the central issue being strategic renewal and repositioning—the foundational assumption is that firms can enact and actively shape their environment (Child 1972)	Strategic choice theory contends that marketing managers' decisions play a tremendous role in a marketing organization's ongoing success or failure in the marketplace, in their product development efforts, and/or in market positioning and segmentation. Strategic choice analysis concerns (1) the relationship between marketing managers and their choices, (2) the dynamics of the marketplace, and (3) the relationship between marketing managers and the marketplace (cf. Child 1997)	Strategic marketing decisions are often made with concern for the marketing organization, rather than marketing channel partners or the marketplace, as the primary driver Marketing organizations are able to adopt and adhere to a specific marketing strategy type which fits their core marketing competencies Strategic choice articulates a "political process, which brings agency and structure into tension and locates then within a significant context … it regards both the relation of agency to structure and to environment as dynamic in nature … the strategic choice approach not only bridges a number of competing perspectives but also adopts a non-deterministic and potentially evolutionary position … strategic choice … locates 'organizational learning' within the context of organizations as socio-political systems" (Child 1997, p. 44)

Systems theory	Systems theory proposes that every system, regardless of its nature (e.g., mechanical, biological, social) is composed of multiple elements that are interconnected (Bertalanffy 1969; Kast and Rosenzweig 1972). In this sense, systems theory seeks to understand scientific phenomena by considering the interdependence of networks of firms and other entities within a larger system (Scott 1981)	Although some systems are closed (i.e., self-contained), marketing organizations are most appropriately viewed as operating within an open system. The open systems perspective stresses the interdependence of the marketing organization and its market environment (Scott 1981)	"All systems are made up of subsystems and are themselves subsumed in larger systems—an arrangement that creates linkages across systems and confounds the attempt to erect clear boundaries around them" (Scott and Davis 2007, p. 96). This systems view lends itself to the study of marketing at multiple levels in the firm Decisions that marketing managers make in an effort to lead their marketing organizations toward prosperity take place within a complicated and complex milieu that requires fine-tuned theorizing to not under-specify marketing strategy modeling
Theory of competitive rationality	The theory of competitive rationality (a.k.a. general theory of oligopolistic competition) "proposes a firm's success depends on the imperfect procedural rationality of its marketing planners … the theory is based on disequilibrium analysis and the marketing skills of economic rivals" to explain how a free market works (Dickson 1992, p. 69)	The original scope of the theory of competitive rationality was developed within a marketing context. Given its marketing foundation, "the basic premise of the theory of competitive rationality is that variation in the response rate of buyers and sellers to changes in supply and demand creates opportunities that can be imperfectly exploited by the motivated, alert, and hustling decision maker" (Dickson 1992, p. 69)	Implicit within the theory of competitive rationality is the notion that marketing organizations which adopt a "clan" culture (i.e., emphasizing cohesiveness, participation, and teamwork; Ouchi 1979) are "more competitive over the long term" and also better suited to operate in an environment described within the boundaries of the theory of competitive rationality (Dickson 1992, p. 78) "The ability to react quickly (agility) is paramount when a firm cannot predict and plan for discontinuities in competitor and buyer behavior … responsiveness can compensate for a firm's imperfect knowledge about the market and its bounded rationality" (Dickson 1992, p. 79)

(continued)

Table 3.2 (continued)

Theory	Original scope	Marketing scope	Marketing insights
Theory of multimarket competition	The theory of multimarket competition (Edwards 1955; Simmel 1950) focuses on interfirm competition and "envisions a firm occupying a potentially unique market domain that is defined by activities in various geographic-product markets … if the market domains of competing firms overlap in multiple geographic-product markets, the firms are engaged in multimarket competition" (Jayachandran et al. 1999, p. 50)	The theory of multimarket competition and its premise of marketing organizations competing against other marketing organizations in multiple domestic and/or international markets (e.g., market segments, countries, regions) envisions the competing marketing organizations occupying unique market positions in the multiple marketplaces, potentially multiple industries, and potentially multiple supply chains	The interaction between multimarket competition and scope economies, through mutual forbearance, can be a mechanism by which marketing organizations can retain the value created by their marketing strategy and scope economies via the avoidance of loss through price competition (Gimeno and Woo 1999) Mutual forbearance (a form of tacit collusion) may reduce the market-level intensity of competition between two marketing organizations when the multimarket contact between them increases, such as when product markets overlap significantly (Jayachandran et al. 1999)
Theory of the growth of the firm	The theory of the growth of the firm is based on a study of industrial firms. "The economic function of such a firm was assumed simply to be that of acquiring and organizing human and other resources in order profitably to supply goods and services to the market … it was defined, therefore, as a collection of resources bound together in an administrative framework, the boundaries of which are determined by the area of administrative coordination and authoritative communication" (Penrose 1959/1995, p. xi)	The theory of the growth of the firm, being rooted mainly in industrial firms, has the most logical connection to marketing channels and supply chains. This theory has served as a logical foundation for the resource-based view, and it addresses acquiring marketing resources (human and others) that can be used by a firm to acquire a position in the marketplace via product and/or service offerings. Interfunctional coordination (administrative coordination) and formal reporting lines among marketing personnel (authoritative communication) are directly applicable to more contemporary marketing organizations and the formation of marketing strategy	Within the confines of the theory of the growth of the firm, it is never the resources a firm possesses that serve as inputs in the production process but only the services that the firm's resources can render. As such, human resources in form of marketing professionals along with other marketing resources create a firm's "services" in Penrose's (1959/1995) terminology; these services form the basis for market action, competitive advantage, and performance Through the marketing organization's experiences comes excess capacity in marketing professionals' knowledge (and possibly in marketing resources) that is subject to marketplace frictions. The result is that the marketing organization seeks to expand in directions that allow for the utilization of the excess marketing resources. Marketing managers are then subsequently faced with the conundrum of how to utilize these marketing resources effectively and efficiently

Theory of the multinational enterprise	The (advantages) theory of the multinational enterprise focuses mainly on the control or governance of value-added activities of firms (Hymer 1960/1976). "Control is desired in order to fully appropriate the returns of certain skills and abilities" (p. 25); "unequal ability of firms is a sufficient condition for foreign operations" (p. 46) but not a necessary one (Hymer 1960/1976). "The firm is a practical institutional device that substitutes for the market. The firm internalizes or supersedes the market. A fruitful approach to our problem is to ask why the market is an inferior method of exploiting the advantage; that is, we look at imperfections in the market" (Hymer 1960/1976, pp. 47–48)	The theory of the multinational enterprise suggests that the scope of the internationally oriented marketing organization rests in control mechanisms and explicit coordination of value-added activities. "It is the market impurity which leads the possessor of the advantage to choose to supersede the market for his advantage" (Hymer 1960/1976, p. 49). Hymer centered on "advantages" throughout his dissertation work; thus, marketing advantages are critically important to the success of marketing organizations internationally and the focus of the internalization of markets is not on reducing costs but instead on exploiting the firm's advantages better	"Hymer's analytical framework involved a focus on the twin advantages that he perceived internalization confers on firms: the ability to reap profits from their advantages, and (including) an increase in market power through the reduction of competition" (Dunning and Pitelis 2008, p. 170) In a marketing sense, the theory of the multinational enterprise "is concerned with the [market] conditions under which an enterprise of one country will be controlled by a firm of another country or enterprises in several countries will be controlled by the same firm … it is a problem of determining the extent of vertical and horizontal integration of firms" (Hymer 1960/1976, pp. 27–28), and their involvement and commitment with the global supply chains that make up their operations

(continued)

Table 3.2 (continued)

Theory	Original scope	Marketing scope	Marketing insights
Transaction cost economics	Transaction cost economics (a.k.a. transaction cost analysis; Rindfleisch and Heide 1997) views the firm as a governance structure (Coase 1937) that focuses on identifying, based on total costs, the exchanges that should be conducted within and outside the scope of a firm's boundaries (Williamson 1975)	Transaction cost economics is rooted in the notion that firms and markets represent alternative governance structures that have different transaction costs; bounded rationality of the marketing organization and market opportunism along with market transactions involving marketing asset specificity and market uncertainty are what glue the firm together as a governance structure	Marketing organizations will engage in the implementation of marketing strategy and accompanying marketing activities when the economic rationale for doing so is clear to them. For example, "if adaptation, performance, evaluation, and safeguarding costs are absent or low, economic actors will favor market governance … if these costs are high enough to exceed the production cost advantages of the market, firms will favor internal organization" (Rindfleisch and Heide 1997, p. 32) Technologies and processes that reduce the total cost of the implementation of a designed marketing strategy, via specific marketing activities, will increase the likelihood of their adoption. Such technologies and/or processes can be implemented "without ownership or complete vertical integration" (Rindfleisch and Heide 1997, p. 32), a refined view of transaction cost economics which was not incorporated in the original framework that suggested that governance was a discrete choice between market exchanges and internal organization

Upper echelons theory	Upper echelons theory integrates literatures from various fields on characteristics of top managers (Hambrick 2005), and develops a foundation that "organizational outcomes—strategic choices and performance levels—are partially predicted by managerial background characteristics" (Hambrick and Mason 1984, p. 193)	Upper echelons theory centers on the characteristics of top marketing managers, their choices for structuring the marketing organization and developing marketing strategy, and the market performance choices and related decisions. The key premise is that major marketing outcomes are largely a function of the decision-making of top marketing executives of the marketing organization	Decisions about marketing organization properties and marketing strategy issues are shaped by past practices and managerial backgrounds of the top marketing managers of the organization More diverse top marketing management teams and integration of top marketing managers within top-level teams in the organization in general can be fruitful to achieve higher degrees of creativity and for the organization to be more proactive about marketing efforts. Such efforts have the potential to adopt an efficient mix of focus on being responsive in the marketplace, being proactive in the marketplace, targeting explicit customer needs, and targeting latent customer needs

professionals (at all levels of hierarchy) own the bulk of the boundary-spanning marketing organization's resources.

- *Adjustment-cost theory of the firm*: This theory has a knowledge focus on adjusting a relationship by making changes. A horizontal expansion should govern the boundary-spanning marketing organization's transfer of any excess strategic marketing resource capacity if it entails frequent and diverse marketing adaptations. If the industry places a premium on flexibility, expand the organization's vertical scope by bringing in parts of the supply chain(s).
- *Service-dominant (SD) logic*: This theory's focus is on "specialized competences (operant resources—knowledge skills)" (Vargo and Lusch 2008, p. 2). The service aspect of SD logic is the provision of the information to or for a consumer who desires it; this could be both an internal and/or an external customer in the boundary-spanning marketing organization.

The classical point of origination for resource-based theories is the theory of the growth of the firm. "The economic function of such a [growth] firm was assumed simply to be that of acquiring and organizing human and other resources in order profitably to supply goods and services to the market … it was defined, therefore, as a collection of resources bound together in an administrative framework, the boundaries of which are determined by the area of administrative coordination and authoritative communication" (Penrose 1959/1995, p. xi). In terms of marketing organizations, the theory of the growth of the firm, rooted mainly in industrial firms, has the most logical connection to marketing channels and supply chains. This theory serves as a rational foundation for the resource-based view, and it addresses acquisition of marketing resources (human and others) that can be used by a firm to establish a position in the marketplace via product and/or service offerings. In addition, interfunctional coordination (administrative coordination) and formal reporting lines among marketing personnel (authoritative communication) are often used when defining aspects of resource-centered marketing organizations and their formation of marketing strategy.

Building on the theory of the growth of the firm, the RBV (Wernerfelt 1984) envisions the firm as a collection of strategic resources which are heterogeneously distributed across firms (Barney 1991) to achieve a sustainable competitive advantage. A key premise of the resource-based view is its direct connection to the performance of the firm via strategic action and competitive advantage (Ketchen et al. 2007). As such, the resource-based view envisions the marketing organization as a bundle of strategic marketing resources that are heterogeneously distributed across organizations and are rooted in an equilibrium-seeking process embedded in a marketplace of perfect competition. A broader but close ally to the resource-based view within the field of marketing is resource-advantage (R-A) theory. R-A theory suggests that the basis for a sustainable competitive advantage resides in the marketing organization's resources and how it structures, bundles, and leverages those marketing resources (Hunt and Morgan 1995). A key difference between the RBV and R-A theory is that R-A theory is rooted in a disequilibrium-seeking process (i.e., the marketing organization is a bundle of marketing resources which is rooted in a disequilibrium-seeking process embedded in a marketplace of less than perfect competition).

One of the theories underlying R-A theory is competence-based theory. In Hunt's view (2000, p. 80), competence-based theory is an "internal factors theory of business strategy" with classical origination in Selznick's (1957) work on "distinctive competence." Competence-based theory was used by Andrews (1971) to refer to what the firm could do particularly well in relation to its competition. It lends itself uniquely to the study of the marketing organization in that it focuses solely on the distinctive competences that make the organization thrive in a competitive environment. Another narrowly defined resource theory is the KBV of the firm. The KBV is mainly a spinoff from the RBV. While competence-based theory focuses on what the firm can do particularly well, the KBV suggests that such competencies and market leadership stem solely from "strategic knowledge"; "the firm is conceptualized as an institution for integrating knowledge" (Grant 1996, p. 109) based on certain learning endeavors (e.g., Bell et al. 2010, 2000). This knowledge focus is a prerequisite for the adjustment-cost theory of the firm. Within the adjustment-cost theory of the firm (Wernerfelt 1997), an organization continually "examines ongoing trading relationships and asks by which process the parties should adjust the relationship by accommodating changes" (Wernerfelt 2005, p. 17).

The most recent addition to these resource theories—service-dominant logic (Vargo and Lusch 2004)—both builds on previous resource theories and uniquely departs from them. In fact, service-dominant logic is not inherently resource focused per se. Rather, service-dominant logic "implies that the goal is to customize offerings, to recognize that the consumer is always a coproducer, and to strive to maximize consumer involvement in the customization to better fit his or her needs" (Vargo and Lusch 2004, p. 12). What ties S-D logic to resource theories is its discussion of specialized competences. Specifically, within service-dominant logic, "*service* is defined as the application of specialized competences (operant resources—knowledge skills), through deeds, processes, and performances for the benefit of another entity or the entity itself" (Vargo and Lusch 2008, p. 2). Based on the theories of strategic marketing resources, the marketing organization is a bundle of marketing resources, created by the strategically unique application of specialized marketing competences, which is rooted in a disequilibrium-seeking process embedded in a marketplace of less than perfect competition.

Marketing Leadership and Decision-Making

Eight of the organization theories in Table 3.2 have an intellectual cluster centered on "leadership and decision making" as they apply to a boundary-spanning marketing organization (i.e., agency theory, bounded rationality theory, game theory, prospect theory, real options theory, strategic choice theory, theory of competitive rationality, and upper echelons theory).

- *Upper echelons theory*: Characteristics of top managers are shaped by past practices and managerial backgrounds, and such practices/backgrounds affect organizational outcomes and choices, including strategic choices and performance levels in the boundary-spanning marketing organization.
- *Strategic choice theory*: This theory involves strategic decisions by marketing managers; the central issue being strategic renewal and repositioning and the foundational assumption being that boundary-spanning marketing organizations can enact and actively shape their environment.
- *Bounded rationality*: This theory addresses ingrained operating procedures and recognizes that it is not possible to understand and analyze all information which is potentially relevant in making firm choices. Managers are limited by the information they have and/or can obtain, emphasizing cognitive limitations of their minds and frame of reference and the time constraint in which they have to make decisions in the boundary-spanning marketing organization.
- *Prospect theory*: This theory addresses making choices involving risk; specifically, it describes how organizations (or people) make choices between alternatives that involve degrees of risk. The issue of "framing" within the confines of prospect theory is generally considered to be inconsistent with economic rationality but is important for the subjective rationale in boundary-spanning marketing organization.
- *Real options theory*: This theory focuses on risk uncertainty and revolves around creating and then exercising or not exercising certain options. Marketing managers should look beyond the net present value of a marketing investment and consider the value of the options offered by such an investment for the boundary-spanning marketing organization.
- *Game theory*: In the "game" of making strategic choices, the focus in such scenarios has been on an individual's success in making strategic choices relative to other players. Subjective-probability judgments or risk assessment by decision makers can be employed to reduce uncertainty as it pertains to the boundary-spanning marketing organization.
- *Agency theory*: In this theory, marketing managers lead instead of owners or top management; the theory explains firm governance by delineating firm owners as principals that hire agents (managers) to carry out the business of operating the boundary-spanning marketing organization.
- *Theory of competitive rationality*: Uniquely qualified leaders can be exploited, meaning that a firm's success is tied to the imperfect procedural rationality of its managers, but responsiveness can make up for the boundary-spanning marketing organization's imperfect knowledge and its bounded rationality.

Marketing leaders in particular are central to the effective and efficient operations of the marketing organization. Marketing outcomes of the organization are directly tied to the strategic decision-making choices made by top-level marketing leaders, as rooted in strategic choice theory (Child 1972) and upper echelons theory (Hambrick and Mason 1984). The characteristics of these marketing managers along with their managerial backgrounds set the tone for what type of marketing decisions will be made (Hambrick 2005), depending on the ingrained operating procedures that the marketing organization has adopted that are boundedly rational (Simon 1945, 1957). In essence, the marketing organization develops techniques, habits, and operating procedures to cope with the often overwhelming amount of information available to marketing leaders—both internal and external. The premise is that marketing leaders have an opportunity to shape both marketing strategy and the external environment in which the firm operates (Child 1972).

Prospect theory suggests that in making strategic choices, marketing leaders evaluate alternatives that involve degrees of risk (Kahneman and Tversky 1979), a premise also addressed by real options theory in the form of risk uncertainty (Myers 1977). An astute marketing leader evaluates potential gains and losses relative to the possibility of exercising available options for implementation. Clearly some marketing leaders are better at the "game" of making strategic choices relative to other organizations in the marketplace (Neumann and Morgenstern 1944). According to agency theory, such decisions also include employing marketing managers to lead the organization's marketing efforts instead of the owners or even top-level management being responsible for marketing leadership (Jensen and Meckling 1976). In these cases, the marketing organization opts to hire marketing specialists who are better suited for and capable of carrying out the marketing activities of the organization. In effect, according to the theory of competitive rationality, the owners of the organization assume that their hiring of a uniquely capable leader creates variation in supply and demand to allow for the development of opportunities that can be imperfectly exploited by their marketing organization (Dickson 1992). Based on the delineation of thought on marketing leadership and decision-making, a top marketing leader in a marketing organization (1) is structurally a part of an involved firm's top management, (2) has authority to make marketing decisions across firm boundaries, and (3) has the capability and capacity to operate throughout the internal–external network.

Network Alliances and Collaborations

As applicable to a boundary-spanning marketing organization, eight of the organization theories in Table 3.2 have an intellectual cluster centered on "network alliances and collaborations" (i.e., behavioral theory of the firm, information economics theory, network theory, resource dependence theory, signaling theory, social capital theory, theory of multimarket competition, and transaction cost economics).

- *Network theory*: Actors, activity links, and resource ties make up a business-focused network; the overall network involves creation of a blend of strong and weak ties between nodes that match the boundary-spanning marketing organization's needs in order to maximize the organization's performance.
- *Theory of multimarket competition*: Boundary-spanning marketing organizations' competition overlaps in multiple geographic markets. Mutual forbearance

(a form of tacit collusion) may reduce the market-level intensity of competition between two organizations when the multimarket contact between them increases, such as when product markets overlap significantly.

- *Social capital theory*: Networks of relationships constitute a valuable resource for the conduct of social affairs. Sensemaking among individuals in boundary-spanning marketing organizations is a key to trust-building in supply chains and market networks.
- *Behavioral theory of the firm*: Organizations should be viewed as consisting of a number of coalitions, and the role of management is to achieve resolution of conflict and uncertainty avoidance across all parts of the boundary-spanning marketing organization.
- *Resource dependence theory*: This theory describes the sources and consequences of power of boundary-spanning marketing organizations embedded in networks of interdependencies and social networks that revolve around the control and dependence on vital external resources in the environment.
- *Information economics theory*: This theory states that information has economic value in networks; it is a branch of microeconomic theory focused on how information affects economic decisions of a boundary-spanning marketing organization.
- *Signaling theory*: This theory involves one firm (the agent) conveying some meaningful information about itself and/or its products and services to another party (the principal). For example, organizations often use costly marketing initiatives to "signal" the type of marketing organization they are and the products that they sell to reduce information asymmetry.
- *Transaction cost economics*: Costs can be used to evaluate exchanges that are internal and external to networks. This theory views the boundary-spanning marketing organization as a governance structure that focuses on identifying, based on total costs, the exchanges that should be conducted within and outside the scope of an organization's boundaries.

Broadly, as a summary of the earlier discussion, network theory involves creating a blend of strong and weak ties between nodes that matches the firm's needs in order to maximize its performance. Network theory describes, explains, and predicts relations among linked entities (e.g., Granovetter 1973; Thorelli 1986). These linked entities consist of actors (i.e., nodes), resource ties, and activity links (Håkansson 1989). Actors control the resources and perform the activities. Activities link resources to each other; an activity occurs when one or several actors combines, develops, exchanges, or creates resources by using other resources. Resources, in the network context, include input goods, financial capital, technology, personnel, and marketing.

Networks are important to effective and efficient operations of the marketing organization. However, networks do not align themselves to just one marketing organization. In fact, the theory of multimarket competition (Edwards 1955; Simmel 1950) stresses this notion by envisioning "a firm occupying a potentially unique market domain that is defined by activities in various geographic-product markets … if the market domains of competing firms overlap in multiple geographic-product markets, the firms are engaged in multimarket competition" (Jayachandran et al. 1999, p. 50). As such, marketing organizations often collaborate with and also compete against other marketing organizations in multiple marketplaces, industries, and supply chains. Social capital theory serves as a good foundation for these potential dual roles of collaboration and competition. Social capital theory's central premise is that networks of relationships constitute a valuable resource for the conduct of social affairs (Homburg et al. 2010b; Nahapiet and Ghoshal 1998, p. 242), providing their members with "the collectivity-owned capital, a 'credential' which entitles them to credit, in the various senses of the word" (Bourdieu 1986, p. 249). Socially, marketing organizations and the marketplace are also composed of people, and the interpersonal behaviors among these people (such as the "credits" and trust they build with each other; cf. Gundlach and Cannon 2010) shape the organization's activities and outcomes. This is where the behavioral theory of the firm provides helpful guidance.

The behavioral theory of the firm holds that organizations should be viewed as consisting of coalitions, and the role of management is to achieve resolution of conflict and uncertainty avoidance within the confines of bounded rationality (Cyert and March 1963/1992). The reasons why the coalitions are created in the network exemplify much of what resource dependence theory encompasses. A significant portion of resource dependence theory is to describe the sources and consequences of power of marketing organizations embedded in networks of interdependencies and social networks that revolve around the control of and dependence on vital external resources in the environment (Pfeffer and Salancik 1978). Similar to the discussion of strategic resources, information (or knowledge in terms of the KBV) serves as the glue that holds together the network and collaborations. By extension, information economics theory can serve to crystallize how information generation and dissemination affect resource allocation and marketing decisions.

A key element is that information has economic value in understanding the network and any individual collaboration between firms (Akerlof 1970; Spence 1974; Stiglitz 1961). Given that information is used, certain firm-level "signals" may play a role as well. Even within internal networks, but certainly within networks external to the firm, some firms use signaling, rooted in signaling theory, to convey meaningful information about themselves and/or their products and services to another party (Spence 1973). Such signaling can create a more advantageous position for a firm in the network, one that leads to advantages in future transactions. For example, it may cost the firm less to engage with another firm in the future if certain signals are sent through the network. As an extension, transaction cost economics can be used to identify, based on total costs, the exchanges that should be conducted within and outside the firm's boundaries (Williamson 1975), i.e., should the internal network and/or collaborations be used to solve a particular need, or should the external network and/or collaborations be invoked to solve the need? Based on the delineation of thought on networks and collaboration, collaboration and competition exist in a marketing organization's networks, both internal and external, and the nature of the collaboration and competition is a function of the power position of the organizations within the network and the information utility which they possess about the core competencies most valuable to the network.

Domestic and Global Marketplace

As applicable to a boundary-spanning marketing organization, eight of the organization theories in Table 3.2 have an intellectual cluster centered on the "domestic and global marketplace" (i.e., contingency theory, eclectic theory of international production, industrial organization, institutional theory, organizational ecology, stakeholder theory, systems theory, and theory of the multinational enterprise). As such, within the boundaries of the marketing organization, the "domestic and global marketplace" permeates the fabric (cf. Webster and White 2010) of these eight theories and serves as a focal point for integration and knowledge insight.

- *Eclectic theory of international production*: This theory provides a three-tiered framework for a boundary-spanning marketing organization to use in determining if it is beneficial to pursue foreign direct investment based on its (potential) advantages in ownership, location, and internalization in the marketplace.
- *Theory of the multinational enterprise*: This theory focuses mainly on the control or governance of value-added activities of firm structures, with control/governance implications for the makeup of the boundary-spanning marketing organization.
- *Institutional theory*: This theory focuses on the processes by which marketplace behavior is established. A boundary-spanning marketing organization tends to be isomorphic to other organizations in its market environment, with organizations resembling each other and behaving similarly over time and with an organization's strategies converging via three mechanisms—coercive, mimetic, and normative.
- *Systems theory*: This theory addresses interdependence of networks of firms in the marketplace. Every system, regardless of its nature (e.g., mechanical, biological, social) is composed of multiple elements that are interconnected; this is especially true in the holistically (cf. Shook et al. 2004) viewed boundary-spanning marketing organization.
- *Stakeholder theory*: There are multiple stakeholders in the firm's marketplace. Managing primary stakeholder relationships (i.e., customers, employees, suppliers, shareholders, communities, and regulators) is essential for the boundary-spanning marketing organization because, at a minimum, not doing so can be detrimental to the achievement of marketing goals and the organization's performance objectives.
- *Industrial organization*: This theory focuses on the strategic behavior of firms, the structure of markets, and their interactions. The market success of an industry in developing products and/or services for customers depends on the collective actions of the firms in the industry, and boundary-spanning marketing organizations within an industry are identical regarding the market resources they control.
- *Organizational ecology*: This theory focuses on understanding the environmental conditions under which organizations emerge, grow, and die. Boundary-spanning marketing organizations that do not adapt their culture, processes, and activities to become appropriately market oriented may be selected out of the population (i.e., marketplace).

- *Contingency theory*: There is flexibility in the firm matching the demands of the marketplace, with different organizational units within a boundary-spanning marketing organization possibly facing different market demands.

The clearest starting point in this category is the eclectic theory of international production (Dunning 1980). It provides a three-tiered framework that can be used to determine whether it is beneficial to pursue a foreign direct investment. This so-called eclectic theory centers on advantages in the areas of (1) ownership (production- or firm-specific advantages such as comparative advantage), (2) location-specific advantages, and (3) market internalization. Regarding market internalization, the logic is to continually evaluate whether it is better for the firm to exploit an international opportunity itself than for it to sign an agreement with a foreign firm (Buckley and Casson 1976, 2011). A parallel can be drawn to the internal–external network focus of the marketing organization (i.e., when should the marketing organization use internal resources, external network resources, or a combination of the two?).

An important issue in this respect can be gleaned from the theory of the multinational enterprise (Hymer 1960/1976). Hymer's theory focuses mainly on the control or governance of value-added activities of firms but helps answer questions regarding when value-added activities should be considered for development relative to the control/governance of such activities (cf. Gilliland et al. 2010). "Control is desired in order to fully appropriate the returns of certain skills and abilities" (Hymer 1960/1976, p. 25); "unequal ability of firms is a sufficient condition for foreign operations" (Hymer 1960/1976, p. 46) but not a necessary one. "The firm is a practical institutional device that substitutes for the market. [In some sense,] the firm internalizes or supersedes the market. An approach to our problem is to ask why the market is an inferior method of exploiting the advantage; that is, we look at imperfections in the market" (Hymer 1960/1976, pp. 47–48). Hymer centers on "advantages" as the main thesis; thus, marketing advantages are critically important to the success of marketing organizations internationally, and the focus of the internalization of markets is not on reducing costs but instead on better exploiting the firm's advantages. This is very similar to the notion of networks in the marketing organization. The focus on networks is not on reducing costs but instead is on gaining a positional advantage for the boundary-spanning marketing organization (cf. Day and Wensley 1988; Hult and Ketchen 2001; Hult et al. 2005).

The cost and other complexities of the organization in the global marketplace can best be portrayed by institutional theory and systems theory. These form the components for the "global identity" of the firm (e.g., Westjohn et al. 2009). "Institutional theory attends to the deeper and more resilient aspects of social structure … it considers the processes by which structures, including schemas, rules, norms, and routines, become established as authoritative guidelines for social behavior … it inquires into how these elements are created, diffused, adopted, and adapted over space and time; and how they fall into decline and disuse" (Scott 2005, p. 461). Systems theory proposes that every system, regardless of its nature (e.g., mechanical, biological, social) is composed of multiple elements that are interconnected

(Bertalanffy 1969; Kast and Rosenzweig 1972). In this sense, systems theory seeks to understand scientific phenomena by considering the interdependence of networks of firms and other entities within a larger system (Scott 1981).

While the environmental and marketplace complexities foundationally rest well in institutional theory and systems theory, stakeholder theory is needed to explain the scope of the "actors" connected to the marketing organization in the marketplace. Stakeholder theory addresses morals and values in managing a firm that has to deal with a multitude of constituent groups other than shareholders (Freeman 1984). As stated earlier, it views the firm as "an organizational entity through which numerous and diverse participants accomplish multiple, and not always entirely congruent, purposes" (Donaldson and Preston 1995, p. 70). Stakeholder theory focuses the marketing organization's efforts on developing and nurturing exchanges with a multitude of constituent groups other than customers and shareholders. As such, the stakeholder approach seeks to broaden a marketing manager's vision of his/her responsibilities beyond being customer and profit oriented (cf. Mitchell et al. 1997).

As soon as the multiple layers of the marketplace are engaged in the scope of what the marketplace entails for the marketing organization, a number of theories become applicable (e.g., industrial organization economics, organizational ecology, contingency theory). Industrial organization theory is rooted in economics and focuses on the strategic behavior of firms, the structure of markets, and their interactions (Bain 1956, 1959; Chamberlin 1933; Mason 1939), ultimately affecting the performance of firms (Schmalensee 1985). For the marketing organization this means that the synergy between the organization's marketing strategy and market structure serves as the essential scope to leverage market performance. The context for such synergy is the marketplace as the environment of business operations. This brings in organizational ecology and contingency theory.

Organizational ecology focuses on understanding the environmental conditions (e.g., market turbulence, technological turbulence, and competitive intensity) under which marketing organizations emerge, grow and change, and die (Hannan and Freeman 1977). Based on Gailbraith (1973), contingency theory suggests that there is no one best way to organize a marketing organization, and each way of organizing is not equally effective. Contingency theory is an outgrowth of systems design and "is guided by the general orienting hypothesis that organizations whose internal features best match the demands of their environments will achieve the best adaptation … [as such], the best way to organize depends on the nature of the environment to which the organization relates" (Scott 2005, p. 89). Thus, contingency theory coupled with IO economics and organizational ecology gives rise to the notion that marketing organizations both influence and are influenced by the marketplace in which they operate. Based on these integrated thoughts on the domestic and global marketplace, marketing organizations, partially due to their internal-external network collaborations and internal-external resource activities, have to operate in internal-external domestic and global networks and attend to the needs and wants of multiple stakeholders and multiple levels of marketplace influences.

Chapter 4
Discussion, Insights, and Implications

The delineation of a theory of the boundary-spanning marketing organization (MOR theory) and the insights gleaned from 31 organization theories for its existence, activities, and viability offer a broad understanding of the boundaries of marketing at the organizational level. With a few exceptions (e.g., resource-based view, network theory), each theory is given a relatively equal importance weighting. Future studies on the marketing organization should consider developing a weighted schema of relevant theories (cf. Miner 2003). For the purpose of this SpringerBrief, an extension and more elaborate version of the Hult (2011b) article in the *Journal of the Academy of Marketing Science*, the cross-fertilization of organization theories clustered into four logical themes creates unique implications that can help advance work on the marketing organization. In elaborating on these implications, a focus on the intellectual clusters of strategic marketing resources, marketing leadership, and decision-making, network alliances and collaborations, and the domestic and global marketplace will continue as the structural roadmap for the discussion.

Strategic Marketing Resources

Several insights for the marketing organization can be advanced by examining the seven organization theories in Table 3.2 that are centered on "strategic marketing resources" (i.e., adjustment-cost theory of the firm, competence-based theory, knowledge-based view of the firm, resource-advantage theory, resource-based view of the firm, service-dominant logic, and theory of the growth of the firm). In some senses, the study of strategic resources is coming full circle; in the beginning it focused on the theory of the growth of the firm (Penrose 1959), and the most recent advancements include the notion of a service-dominant logic in marketing (Vargo and Lusch 2004).

Within the confines of the theory of the growth of the firm, it is never the resources a firm possesses that serve as inputs in the production process but only the services

G.T.M. Hult, *Boundary-Spanning Marketing Organization: A Theory and Insights from 31 Organization Theories*, SpringerBriefs in Business 20,
DOI 10.1007/978-1-4614-3819-9_4, © Academy of Marketing Science 2011

that the firm's resources can render. Marketing professionals, along with other marketing resources, create a firm's "services" in Penrose's (1959) terminology; these services form the basis for market action, competitive advantage, and performance. In parallel, Vargo and Lusch (2004, p. 9) state that "the use of knowledge as the basis for competitive advantage can be extended to the entire 'supply chain,' or service-provision chain … we argue that the primary flow [in the supply chain] is information; *service* is the provision of the information to (or use of the information for) a consumer who desires it, with or without an accompanying appliance." The focus is on the "co-creation of value, process orientation, and relationships" (Merz et al. 2009, p. 329). This "service" focus is also supported within the resource-based view. Marketing resources have only potential value, with the value ultimately being realized (or not) via organizational actions and behaviors (Ketchen et al. 2007). As such, strategic resources need to be converted into action before affecting an organization's performance.

However, certain actions lead to excess capacity. Sometimes through the marketing organization's experiences comes excess capacity in professionals' knowledge (and possibly in marketing resources) that is subject to marketplace frictions. The result is that the marketing organization seeks to expand in directions that allow for the utilization of these excess resources. Marketing managers are then subsequently faced with the conundrum of how to utilize the resources effectively and efficiently. To achieve effectiveness and efficiency, the service-dominant logic argues for "an increased focus on operant resources and specifically process management" (Vargo and Lusch 2004, p. 10). This process focus overlaps the view of the "marketing process organization" by Moorman and Rust (1999) and the business process focus by Srivastava et al. (1999). At the same time, at the foundational level, it is important to realize that firms differ even within an industry (Wernerfelt 1984). "The differences occur in the firms' resources, and the main theory is that a firm's strategy should depend on its resources—if a firm is good at something, the firm should try to use it" (Wernerfelt 2005, p. 17). The assumption is that what a marketing organization is good at is readily identifiable and that the organization can adapt as needed. This may or may not be true.

The marketing organization's use of strategic marketing resources is correlated with a need for frequent and diverse marketing adaptations. A horizontal expansion should govern the marketing organization's transfer of any excess strategic marketing resource capacity if it entails frequent and diverse marketing adaptations. However, such a generic strategy is not necessarily the right strategic fit for all marketing organizations. If the industry places a premium on flexibility in the marketing organization's interactions with its supply chains, the adjustment-cost theory suggests that the organization should expand its vertical scope by bringing in parts of the supply chain(s). Whether the expansion is horizontal or vertical, resource-advantage theory stresses that marketing productivity and economic growth are furthered through both the efficient allocation of scarce tangible marketing resources and the creation of new intangible, and tangible marketing resources. The key is that strategic marketing practices and operations can provide a competitive advantage for all marketing organizations in the marketplace. R-A theory implies that this is not a zero-sum game. Instead, there are net gains that can be realized in strategic resources and the accompanying outputs.

One such example is in strategic knowledge development and use (e.g., Hurley and Hult 1998). For example, there is an implicit assumption that there is value in production gains and that they can be realized through marketing professionals specializing in knowledge acquisition and organizational memory storage. Development of marketing strategy and the accompanying product and service assortment requires the input and coordination of a wide range of specialized market and marketing knowledge. If the primary productive resource of the marketing organization is market and/or marketing knowledge, and if knowledge resides in individual marketing professionals, then it is the marketing professionals (at all levels of hierarchy) who own the bulk of the marketing organization's resources. However, one person possessing the knowledge does not prevent another marketing manager from possessing the same knowledge. In fact, it is critically important, at times, that marketing capabilities permeate the fabric of the marketing organization. The "essence of [marketing] strategy lies in creating tomorrow's competitive advantages faster than competitors mimic the ones you possess today," which implies that marketing organizations should invest in core competencies given that "an organization's capacity to improve existing skills and learn new ones is the most defensible competitive advantage of all" (Hamel and Prahalad 1989, p. 69).

Marketing Leadership and Decision-Making

Marketing leadership and decision making by marketing leaders are often studied within, for example, a sales management context but more seldom within the confines of marketing organizations that span firm boundaries. Given the composition of the marketing organization, studying marketing leadership and decision making that are beyond the scope of the marketing department or function is critical to better understanding the management of a marketing organization. Eight organization theories in Table 3.2 are centered on "leadership and decision making" as they apply to the theory of the boundary-spanning marketing organization (i.e., agency theory, bounded rationality, game theory, prospect theory, real options theory, strategic choice theory, theory of competitive rationality, and upper echelons theory). Certain aspects of these theories have implications for the marketing organization, leadership, and decision making.

The clearest implication is tied to upper echelons theory. Decisions about the marketing organization's properties (and marketing strategy issues) are shaped by past practices and managerial backgrounds of top marketing managers. More diverse top marketing management teams and integration of marketing managers within top level teams can be fruitful to achieve higher degrees of creativity and for the organization to be more proactive about marketing efforts. Such efforts have the potential to result in an efficient mix of focus on being responsive in the marketplace, being proactive in the marketplace, targeting explicit customer needs, and targeting latent customer needs. The assumption is that the marketing organizations are able to adopt and adhere to a specific marketing strategy type which fits their core marketing competencies and makes them competitive in the marketplace. On the other hand, a limitation of having a strategic choice is that decisions are often made with concern for the firm, rather than marketing channel partners or the marketplace, as the primary driver. To be effective, such decision making needs to change when the unit of analysis shifts to the marketing organization since it spans the boundaries of traditional firms.

This shift in unit of analysis (i.e., from the marketing department or the traditional firm to the marketing organization) has bounded rationality implications. Historically, the rationality of marketing managers is limited by the information they have and/or can obtain the cognitive limitations of their minds and frames of reference, and the time constraint in which they have to make decisions to develop the marketing organization and/or its marketing strategy. Marketing managers are "intendedly rational, but only boundedly so" (Simon 1945/1997, p. 88), which means that rational behavior and limits of rationality are the basic premises for marketing managers in developing marketing organizations and forming marketing strategy. However, rational thoughts would not necessarily lend credence to the boundaries of a marketing organization that includes both internal and external dimensions of traditional firms. This is where prospect theory can be helpful. Prospect theory leaves it up to the marketing manager to subjectively frame a marketing outcome or transaction. Such framing affects the marketing utility that can be expected to be obtained by the marketing organization. The issue of "framing," within the confines of prospect theory, is generally considered to be inconsistent with economic rationality but is important for the subjective rationale within the notion of "marketing rationality" as a part of the theory of the boundary-spanning marketing organization.

Rationality also stresses that value is "at the end of the tunnel." Marketing managers should look beyond the net present value of a marketing investment and consider the value of the options offered by such an investment. In this context, a real option has as its underlying marketing asset the total value of the marketing project, with the cost being the investment required to obtain the asset and the time to maturity being reflected in the period in which the marketing manager can defer the investment before it expires. The decision making created by the notion of real options is in essence a marketing game (i.e., a best guess, based on available information, that the net present value of a project will be high enough to warrant an investment). More traditionally, game theory can be used in the marketing organization to develop marketing strategy through gaining a better theoretical understanding of decision-making choices and possible outcomes in potential give-and-take and/or competitive market situations. The outcomes of possible scenarios can be depicted in game matrices, with optimal solutions being determined based on a variety of different assumptions.

An important limitation of game theory, however, is the lack of rational behavior and/or intentions on the part of some marketing leaders. In concert, a central element of agency theory is the so-called agency problem. It arises when the interests of the marketing leader and owner(s) of the firm diverge. Due to information asymmetry between marketing leaders and owner(s), the possibility exists that the leaders will act opportunistically, in their own interests, rather than in the owners' interests. Such differences are often more significant in the global marketplace. "Because cross-cultural differences magnify the problems of uncertainty, asymmetric information, and monitoring, efficient agency relationships can be even more difficult to achieve in multinational markets than in domestic markets" (Bergen et al. 1992, p. 18). The theory of competitive rationality would suggest that a solution to such problems is agility. "The ability to react quickly (agility) is paramount when a firm cannot predict and plan for discontinuities in competitor and buyer behavior...responsiveness can compensate for a firm's imperfect knowledge about the market and its bounded rationality" (Dickson 1992, p. 79).

Network Alliances and Collaborations

Internal and external network alliances and collaborations make marketing organizations complex but also unique in terms of the strategic resources that can be developed and utilized. As applied within the context of marketing organizations, eight organization theories in Table 3.2 focus on "network alliances and collaborations" (i.e., behavioral theory of the firm, information economics theory, network theory, resource dependence theory, signaling theory, social capital theory, theory of multimarket competition, and transaction cost economics). An integrative examination of the eight theories gives rise to a number of insights and research implications. The logical starting point is network theory. At its most basic level, actors (e.g., marketing organizations, marketing professionals), activity links (e.g., forming supply chains involving multiple actors), and resource ties (e.g., joint market orientation efforts among marketing organizations) bind the network together. In these networks, strong and weak ties are formed on a case-by-case basis rather than strategically across marketing organizations. Importantly, often a blend of strong and weak ties that matches the organization's marketing needs should be created proactively and perhaps strategically in order to maximize performance for each organization within the network.

These strong and weak network ties could be resource dependent or transaction dependent. Marketing organizations will engage in the implementation of marketing strategy and accompanying marketing activities within a network when the economic rationale for doing so is clear to them. For example, "if adaptation, performance, evaluation, and safeguarding costs are absent or low, economic actors will favor market governance ... if these costs are high enough to exceed the production cost advantages of the market, firms will favor internal organization" (Rindfleisch and Heide 1997, p. 32). Technologies and processes that reduce the total cost of the implementation of a designed marketing strategy, via specific marketing activities, will increase the likelihood of their adoption. Such technologies and/or processes can be implemented "without ownership or complete vertical integration" (Rindfleisch and Heide 1997, p. 32). This is a refined view of transaction cost economics that was not incorporated in the original framework, which suggested that governance was a discrete choice between market exchanges and internal organization. On the other hand, a marketing organization's ability to implement marketing strategy may be constrained when it is dependent on other organizations within its networks. Specifically, the external environment contains limited resources, so marketing organizations must learn to hold back at times in developing marketing strategy that is resource dependent and trust each other if they are going to coexist successfully over time (or develop new intangible and/or tangible resources; Hunt and Morgan 1995).

To work, creating new marketing resources, as opposed to simply using existing ones, has to be an ingrained value and belief in the fabric of the organization. The marketing organization operates within the confines of "imperfect environmental matching, the observation that the rules, forms, and practices used by economic actors are not uniquely determined by the demands of the environmental setting in which they arise" (Cyert and March 1963/1992, p. 215). In some sense, then, the marketing organization operates within the confines of "unresolved conflict, the assumption that economic organizations involve multiple actors with conflicting interests not entirely resolved by employment contracts" (Cyert and March 1963/1992, p. 215). Such a behavioral theory of the firm inherently places a marketing organization at a disadvantage in the marketplace in terms of creating a net gain of marketing resources for all players in the industry. The dynamics of the network are also likely to be skewed toward being competitive instead of collaborative in creating new resources. This is not to say that the network actors are not collaborative, but the sophisticated level to which marketing organizations have to elevate their strategic thinking to create new marketing resources for the sake of the network and industry, and not just their own firm, needs additional research.

The interaction between multimarket competition and scope economies, through mutual forbearance, can be a mechanism by which marketing organizations can retain the value created by their marketing resources (Gimeno and Woo 1999). Mutual forbearance (a form of tacit collusion) may reduce the market-level intensity of competition between two marketing organizations when the multimarket contact between them increases, such as when product markets overlap significantly (Jayachandran et al. 1999). The idea, though, is that mutual forbearance could present an opportunity even within a marketing organization's network (especially in the global marketplace). In essence, a mixture of shared and organization-level goals, values, and experiences across firms (even competitors) drive marketing strategy-making, which leads to superior success. Sensemaking, as a form of positive social capital (cf. De Clercq et al. 2009) among individuals in and between organizations, is a key to building trust in these competitive and collaborative networks.

While collaborative networks typically work out their arrangements via commitment and trust (Morgan and Hunt 1994), competitive networks which thrive off each other need different mechanisms. Information economics theory and signaling theory provide such a platform. In a situation of information asymmetry (which is typically the case between competitors), marketing organizations can signal to the marketplace important aspects of their organization, such as new product announcements (Homburg et al. 2009), thus transferring information to the organization's stakeholders (most notably, to its customers) and competitors, and resolving the information asymmetry. At the same time, it is difficult for competitors to know which marketing organizations are genuinely committed to business practices with which they associate. In this context, some organizations use costly marketing initiatives to "signal" the type of organization they are to others who would benefit from such knowledge or whom the organization would benefit from being closer linked to in the marketplace.

Domestic and Global Marketplace

The nuances that differentiate the "domestic and global marketplace" are a matter of scale, scope, and complexities (e.g., Hult et al. 2008a, b; Kirca et al. 2011, 2012a, b; Yip and Hult 2012). Marketing organizations scan the global strategy opportunities in the marketplace (e.g., Lukas et al. 2001), relative to what the organization can offer and what the industry allows (e.g., Yip and Hult 2012), to find a customer segment match or strategic fit (cf. Slater et al. 2006, 2007). This match may be domestic or global and involve one or multiple customer segments (cf. Brady et al. 2005; Chabowski et al. 2010; Cronin et al. 2000). Eight of the organization theories in Table 3.2 focus on issues that are relevant for the marketplace (i.e., contingency theory, eclectic theory of international production, industrial organization, institutional theory, organizational ecology, stakeholder theory, systems theory, and theory of the multinational enterprise). A component of the marketplace focus is Hymer's theory of the multinational enterprise. "Hymer's analytical framework focused on the twin advantages internalization confers on firms: the ability to reap profits from their advantages, and (including) an increase in market power through the reduction of competition" (Dunning and Pitelis 2008, p. 170). In a marketing sense, Hymer's theory "is concerned with the [market] conditions under which an enterprise of one country will be controlled by a firm of another country or enterprises in several countries will be controlled by the same firm … it is a problem of determining the extent of vertical and horizontal integration of firms" (Hymer 1960/1976, pp. 27–28).

The marketing organization's advantage is often intangible but can usually be transferred within the organization at a relatively low cost (e.g., technology, brand name, economies of scale). This market and/or marketing advantage gives rise to greater revenues and/or lower costs that can offset the costs of operating at a distance in a global location. To be successful, the marketing organization should use select foreign factors in connection with its home country-specific advantages in order to earn full rents. Specifically, the location advantages of different countries are keys to determining which country or countries will become host countries for the multinational marketing organization. Overall, the marketing organization has a number of choices of entry mode into global markets, beginning with the market (arm's length transactions) and spanning to the hierarchy (wholly owned subsidiary). As such, the marketing organization, in this context, selects internalization when the market does not exist or when it functions poorly.

In fact, often the marketing organization operates within a framework of continual contingency planning when engaging globally. For example, different subunits within a marketing organization may face different market demands. To tackle these different market conditions, organizations need to create specialized subunits with differing structural features—for example, different levels of formalization and planning time horizon. With increased variation in global market conditions, an organization's structure needs to be more differentiated to face all potential challenges in the marketplace. Differentiation is a way to operate effectively and efficiently within the global marketplace system, which includes numerous domestic markets and submarkets. "All systems are made up of subsystems and are themselves subsumed in larger systems—an arrangement that creates linkages across systems and confounds the attempt to erect clear boundaries around them" (Scott and Davis 2007, p. 96). As such, decisions that marketing managers make in an effort to lead their marketing organizations toward prosperity, especially globally, take place within a complicated and complex milieu that requires fine-tuned theorizing to not under-specify marketing strategy-making.

In fact, to attain legitimacy, an organization tends to be isomorphic to other organizations in its market environment, with organizations resembling each other and behaving similarly over time (e.g., Dacin 1997). As such, the way a particular marketing organization interacts with and treats its customers influences other organizations' interactions with their customers. These influences are important for both the evolution of the marketplace and the evolution of each marketing organization. In particular, new marketing organizations and new organizational forms (e.g., vertically and/or horizontally integrated) will arise that are well suited to contemporary marketing strategy, networks, and marketplaces. Marketing organizations that do not adapt their culture, processes, and activities to become appropriately market oriented may be selected out of the marketplace. Even IO economics supports this collective nature of market and organizational development.

Specifically, in line with the structure-conduct-performance approach, the success of an industry in developing products for customers depends on the collective actions of the organizations in the industry. In turn, the market actions of the marketing organizations depend on the actors who determine the competitiveness of the market. Importantly, per IO economics, marketing organizations within an industry are identical regarding the market resources they control. However, should resource heterogeneity develop, it will likely be temporary, given that market resources are highly mobile. As such, homogeneity of marketing strategies among organizations competing in the same industry exists since, for example, marketing actions taken by an organization are easily observable and duplicated by other organizations. As such, we can speculate that perhaps this also means that a theory of the boundary-spanning marketing organization, with its primary stakeholders (i.e., customers, employees, suppliers, shareholders, communities, and regulators) and secondary stakeholders (e.g., media, special interest groups), ultimately will include each other as stakeholders (i.e., competitors internal and external to the marketing organization's primary industry).

> The boundary-spanning marketing organization is defined as an entity encompassing marketing activities that cross a firm's internal and external customer value–creating business processes and networks for the purposes of satisfying the needs and wants of important stakeholders.

References

Achrol, R.S. 1991. Evolution of the marketing organization: new forms for dynamic environments. *Journal of Marketing* 55: 77–93.

Achrol, R.S., and P. Kotler. 1999. Marketing in the network economy. *Journal of Marketing* 63(Special Issue): 146–163.

Akerlof, G.A. 1970. The market for lemons: quality uncertainty and the market mechanism. *Quarterly Journal of Economics* 84(3): 488–500.

Anderson, E.M. 1985. The salesperson as outside agent or employee: a transaction cost analysis. *Marketing Science* 4: 234–254.

Anderson, J.C., H. Håkansson, and J. Johanson. 1994. Dyadic business relationships within a business network context. *Journal of Marketing* 58: 1–15.

Andrews, K. 1971. *The concept of corporate strategy*. Homewood, IL: Richard D. Irwin.

Arrow, K.J. 1969. The organization of economic activity: issues pertinent to the choice of market versus nonmarket allocation. In *The analysis and evaluation of public expenditure: the PPB system*. Vol. 1, U.S. Joint Economic Committee, 91st Congress, 1st Session, 59–73. Washington, DC: U.S. Government Printing Office.

Atuahene-Gima, K., S.F. Slater, and E.M. Olson. 2005. The contingent value of responsive and proactive market orientations for new product program performance. *Journal of Product Innovation Management* 22(6): 464–482.

Aurier, P., and G. N'Goala. 2010. The differing and mediating roles of trust and relationship commitment in service relationship maintenance and development. *Journal of the Academy of Marketing Science* 38(3): 303–325.

Bain, J.S. 1956. *Barriers to new competition*. Cambridge, MA: Harvard University Press.

Bain, J.S. 1959. *Industrial organization*. New York: Wiley.

Barney, J.B. 1991. Firm resources and sustained competitive advantage. *Journal of Management* 17(1): 99–120.

Bell, S.J., B. Menguc, and R.E. Widing. 2010. Salesperson learning, organizational learning, and retail store performance. *Journal of the Academy of Marketing Science* 38(2): 187–201.

Bergen, M., S. Dutta, and O.C. Walker Jr. 1992. Agency relationships in marketing: a review of the implications and applications of agency and related theories. *Journal of Marketing* 56: 1–24.

Birnbaum, P.H. 1985. Political strategies of regulated organizations as functions of context and fear. *Strategic Management Journal* 6(2): 135–150.

Blocker, C.P., D.J. Flint, M.B. Myers, and S.F. Slater. 2011. Proactive customer orientation and its role for creating customer value in global markets. *Journal of the Academy of Marketing Science* 39(2): 216–233.

Bourdieu, P. 1986. The forms of capital. In *Handbook of theory and research for the sociology of education*, ed. J.G. Richardson, 241–258. New York: Greenwood.

G.T.M. Hult, *Boundary-Spanning Marketing Organization: A Theory and Insights from 31 Organization Theories*, SpringerBriefs in Business 20, DOI 10.1007/978-1-4614-3819-9, © Academy of Marketing Science 2011

Boyer, K.K., and G.T.M. Hult. 2005a. Customer behavior in an online ordering application: a decision scoring model. *Decision Sciences* 36(4): 569–598.

Boyer, K.K., and G.T.M. Hult. 2005b. Extending the supply chain: integrating operations and marketing in the online grocery industry. *Journal of Operations Management* 23(6): 642–661.

Boyer, K.K., and G.T.M. Hult. 2006. Customer behavioral intentions for online purchases: an examination of fulfillment method and customer experience level. *Journal of Operations Management* 24(2): 124–147.

Brady, M.K., G.A. Knight, J.J. Cronin Jr., G.T.M. Hult, and B.D. Keillor. 2005. Removing the contextual lens: a multinational, multi-setting comparison of service evaluation models. *Journal of Retailing* 81(3): 215–230.

Brown, S.L., and K.M. Eisenhardt. 1995. Product development: past research, present findings, and future directions. *Academy of Management Review* 20(2): 343–378.

Buckley, P.J., and M.C. Casson. 1976. *The future of the multinational enterprise*. London: Macmillan.

Buckley, P.J., and M.C. Casson. 2011. Marketing and the multinational: extending internalization theory. *Journal of the Academy of Marketing Science* 39(4): 492–508.

Chabowski, B.R., G.T.M. Hult, T. Kiyak, and J.A. Mena. 2010. The structure of JIBS' social network and the relevance of intra-country variation: a typology for future research. *Journal of International Business Studies* 41(5): 925–934.

Chabowski, B.R., G.T.M. Hult, and J.A. Mena. 2011. The retailing literature as a basis for franchising research: using intellectual structure to advance theory. *Journal of Retailing* 87(3): 269–284.

Chamberlin, E.H. 1933. *Theory of monopolistic competition*. Cambridge, MA: Harvard University Press.

Chandler, A.D. 1990. *Scale and scope: the dynamics of industrial capitalism*. Cambridge, MA: Harvard University Press.

Child, J. 1972. Organizational structure, environment, and performance—the role of strategic choice. *Sociology* 6: 1–22.

Child, J. 1997. Strategic choice in the analysis of action, structure, organizations and environment: retrospect and prospect. *Organization Studies* 18(1): 43–76.

Clarkson, M. 1995. A stakeholder framework for analyzing and evaluating corporate social performance. *Academy of Management Review* 20(1): 92–117.

Coase, R.H. 1937. The nature of the firm. *Economica* 4(16): 386–405.

Coase, R.H. 1960. The problem of social costs. *Journal of Law and Economics* 3(1): 1–44.

Connelly, B.L., D.J. Ketchen Jr., and S.F. Slater. 2010. Toward a "theoretical toolbox" for sustainability research in marketing. *Journal of the Academy of Marketing Science* 39(1): 86–100.

Craighead, C.W., G.T.M. Hult, and D.J. Ketchen Jr. 2009. The effects of innovation-cost strategy, knowledge, and action in the supply chain on firm performance. *Journal of Operations Management* 27(5): 405–421.

Craighead, C.W., D.J. Ketchen Jr., K.S. Dunn, and G.T.M. Hult. 2011. Addressing common method variance: guidelines for survey research on information technology, operations, and supply chain management. *IEEE Transactions on Engineering Management* 58(2): 578–588.

Cronin, J.J., M.K. Brady, and G.T.M. Hult. 2000. Assessing the effects of quality, value, and customer satisfaction on consumer behavioral intentions in service environments. *Journal of Retailing* 76(2): 193–218.

Cyert, R.M., and J.G. March. 1963/1992. *A behavioral theory of the firm*. Malden, MA: Blackwell.

Dacin, M.T. 1997. Isomorphism in context: the power and prescription of institutional norms. *Academy of Management Journal* 40(1): 46–81.

Dant, R.P., and P.L. Schul. 1992. Conflict resolution processes in contractual channels of distribution. *Journal of Marketing* 56 (January): 38–54.

Day, G.S. 1994. The capabilities of market-driven organizations. *Journal of Marketing* 58: 37–52.

Day, G.S. 1999. Misconceptions about market orientation. *Journal of Market-Focused Management* 4(1): 5–16.

Day, G.S. 2011. Closing the marketing capabilities gap. *Journal of Marketing* 75(4): 183–195.

Day, G.S., and L. Fahey. 1988. Valuing market strategies. *Journal of Marketing* 52(3): 45–57.

Day, G.S., and R. Wensley. 1988. Assessing advantage: a framework for diagnosing competitive superiority. *Journal of Marketing* 52: 1–20.

De Clercq, D., N. Thongpapanl, and D. Dimov. 2009. When good conflict gets better and bad conflict becomes worse: the role of social capital in the conflict-innovation relationship. *Journal of the Academy of Marketing Science* 37(3): 283–297.

di Benedetto, C.A. 1987. Modeling rationality in marketing decision-making with game theory. *Journal of the Academy of Marketing Science* 15(Winter): 22–32.

Dickson, P.R. 1992. Toward a general theory of competitive rationality. *Journal of Marketing* 56(1): 69–83.

DiMaggio, P.J., and W.W. Powell. 1983. The iron cage revisited: institutional isomorphism and collective rationality in organizational fields. *American Sociological Review* 48: 147–160.

Donaldson, T., and L.E. Preston. 1995. The stakeholder theory of the corporation: concepts, evidence, and implications. *Academy of Management Review* 20(1): 65–91.

Dunning, J.H. 1980. Toward an eclectic theory of international production—some empirical tests. *Journal of International Business Studies* 11(1): 9–31.

Dunning, J.H., and C.N. Pitelis. 2008. Stephen Hymer's contribution to international business scholarship: an assessment and extension. *Journal of International Business Studies* 39(1): 167–176.

Edwards, C.D. 1955. Conglomerate bigness as a source of power. In *Business concentration and price policy*, National Bureau of Economic Research conference report, 331–352. Princeton, NJ: Princeton University Press.

Eesley, C., and M.J. Lenox. 2006. Firm responses to secondary stakeholder action. *Strategic Management Journal* 27(8): 765–781.

Esper, T.L., A.E. Ellinger, T.P. Stank, D.J. Flint, and M. Moon. 2010. Demand and supply integration: a conceptual framework of value creation through knowledge management. *Journal of the Academy of Marketing Science* 38(1): 5–18.

Fayol, H. 1916. *Administration industrielle et generale*. Paris: Dunod.

Ferrell, O.C., T.L. Gonzalez-Padron, G.T.M. Hult, and I. Maignan. 2010. From market orientation to stakeholder orientation. *Journal of Public Policy and Marketing* 29(1): 93–96.

Freeman, R.E. 1984. *Strategic management: a stakeholder approach*. Marshfield, MA: Pitman Publishing.

Gailbraith, J.R. 1973. *Designing complex organizations*. Reading, MA: Addison Wesley.

Gaski, J.F. 1984. The theory of power and conflict in channels of distribution. *Journal of Marketing* 48 (Summer): 9–29.

Gilliland, D.I., D.C. Bello, and G.T. Gundlach. 2010. Control-based channel governance and relative dependence. *Journal of the Academy of Marketing Science* 38(4): 441–455.

Gimeno, J., and C. Woo. 1999. Multimarket contact, economics of scope, and firm performance. *Academy of Management Journal* 42: 239–259.

Granovetter, M. 1973. The strength of weak ties. *The American Journal of Sociology* 78(6): 1360–1380.

Grant, R.M. 1996. Toward a knowledge-based theory of the firm. *Strategic Management Journal* 17(Winter Special Issue): 109–122.

Grant, R.M. 2002. The knowledge-based view of the firm. In *The strategic management of intellectual capital and organizational knowledge*, ed. C.W. Choo and N. Bontis, 133–148. Oxford: Oxford University Press.

Gundlach, G.T., and J.P. Cannon. 2010. Trust but verify? The performance implications of verification strategies in trusting relationships. *Journal of the Academy of Marketing Science* 38(4): 399–417.

Håkansson, H. 1987. *Industrial technological development—a network approach*. Kent, England: Croom Helm, Ltd.

Håkansson, H. 1989. *Corporate technological behaviour*. Worchester, England: Billing & Sons, Ltd.

Håkansson, H. 1992. Evolution processes in industrial networks. In *Industrial networks—a new view of reality*, ed. B. Axelsson and G. Easton. London, England: Routledge.

Håkansson, H., and J. Johanson. 1984. A model of industrial networks. In *Industrial networks—a new view of reality*, ed. B. Axelsson and G. Easton. London, England: Routledge.

Håkansson, H., and C. Östberg. 1975. Industrial marketing—an organizational problem. *Industrial Marketing Management* 4(2/3): 113–123.

Hanvanich, S., K. Sivakumar, and G.T.M. Hult. 2006. The relationship of learning and memory with organizational performance: the moderating role of turbulence. *Journal of the Academy of Marketing Science* 34(4): 600–612.

Hambrick, D.C. 2005. Upper echelons theory: origins, twists and turns, and lessons learned. In *Great minds in management: the process of theory development*, ed. K.G. Smith and M.A. Hitt, 109–127. Oxford: Oxford University Press.

Hambrick, D.C., and P.A. Mason. 1984. Upper echelons: the organization as a reflection of its top managers. *Academy of Management Review* 9(2): 193–206.

Hamel, G., and C.K. Prahalad. 1989. Strategic intent. *Harvard Business Review* 83: 63–76.

Hannan, M.T., and J.H. Freeman. 1977. The population ecology of organizations. *The American Journal of Sociology* 82(5): 929–964.

Heide, J.B., and G. John. 1988. The role of dependence balancing in safeguarding transaction-specific assets in conventional channels. *Journal of Marketing* 52(1): 20–35.

Hess, A.M., and F.T. Rothearmel. 2011. When are assets complementary? Star scientists, strategic alliances, and innovation in the pharmaceutical industry. *Strategic Management Journal* 32: 895–909.

Hillebrand, B., J.J. Nijholt, and E.J. Nijssen. 2011. Exploring CRM effectiveness: an institutional theory perspective. *Journal of the Academy of Marketing Science* 39(1): 592–608.

Homburg, C., T. Bornemann, and D. Totzek. 2009. Preannouncing pioneering versus follower products: what should the message be? *Journal of the Academy of Marketing Science* 37(3): 310–327.

Homburg, C., A. Furst, and J.-K. Prigge. 2010a. A customer perspective of product eliminations: how the removal of products affects customers and business relationships. *Journal of the Academy of Marketing Science* 38(5): 531–549.

Homburg, C., and C. Pflesser. 2000. A multiple-layer model of market-oriented organizational culture: measurement issues and performance outcomes. *Journal of Marketing Research* 37: 449–462.

Homburg, C., J. Wieseke, and C. Kuehnl. 2010b. Social influence on salespeople's adoption of sales technology: a multilevel analysis. *Journal of the Academy of Marketing Science* 38(2): 159–168.

Hult, G.T.M. 1995. *An international organizational learning study of the internal marketing system*. Unpublished doctoral dissertation, The University of Memphis.

Hult, G.T.M. 1998. Managing the international strategic sourcing function as a market-driven organizational learning system. *Decision Sciences* 29(1): 193–216.

Hult, G.T.M. 2003. An integration of thoughts on knowledge management. *Decision Sciences* 34(2): 189–195.

Hult, G.T.M. 2011. Market-focused sustainability: market orientation plus! *Journal of the Academy of Marketing Science* 39(1): 1–6.

Hult, G., and M. Tomas. 2011. Toward a theory of the boundary-spanning marketing organization and insights from 31 organization theories. *Journal of the Academy of Marketing Science* 39(4): 509–536.

Hult, G.T.M., K.K. Boyer, and D.J. Ketchen Jr. 2007a. Quality, operational logistics strategy, and repurchase intentions: a profile deviation analysis. *Journal of Business Logistics* 28(2): 105–132.

Hult, G.T.M., and B.R. Chabowski. 2008. Sourcing research as an intellectual network of ideas. *Decision Sciences* 39(3): 323–335.

Hult, G.T.M., C.W. Craighead, and D.J. Ketchen Jr. 2010. Risk uncertainty and supply chain decisions: a real options perspective. *Decision Sciences* 41(3): 435–458.
Hult, G.T.M., R.F. Hurley, L.C. Giunipero, and E.L. Nichols Jr. 2000. Organizational learning in global purchasing: a model and test of internal users and corporate buyers. *Decision Sciences* 31(2): 293–325.
Hult, G.T.M., and D.J. Ketchen Jr. 2001. Does market orientation matter? A test of the relationship between positional advantage and performance. *Strategic Management Journal* 22(9): 899–906.
Hult, G.T.M., D.J. Ketchen Jr., and M. Arrfelt. 2007b. Strategic supply chain management: improving performance through a culture of competitiveness and knowledge management. *Strategic Management Journal* 28(10): 1035–1052.
Hult, G.T.M., D.J. Ketchen Jr., S.T. Cavusgil, and R. Calantone. 2006. Knowledge as a strategic resource in supply chains. *Journal of Operations Management* 24(5): 458–475.
Hult, G.T.M., D.J. Ketchen Jr., D.A. Griffith, B.R. Chabowski, M.K. Hoffman, B.J. Dykes, W.A. Pollitte, and S.T. Cavusgil. 2008a. An assessment of the measurement of performance in international business research. *Journal of International Business Studies* 39(6): 1064–1080.
Hult, G.T.M., D.J. Ketchen Jr., D.A. Griffith, C.A. Finnegan, T.L. Padron-Gonzalez, F.N. Harmancioglu, Y. Huang, M.B. Talay, and S.T. Cavusgil. 2008b. An assessment of cross-cultural data equivalence in international business research. *Journal of International Business Studies* 39(6): 1027–1044.
Hult, G.T.M., D.J. Ketchen Jr., and E.L. Nichols Jr. 2002. An examination of cultural competitiveness and order fulfillment cycle time within supply chains. *Academy of Management Journal* 45(3): 577–586.
Hult, G.T.M., D.J. Ketchen Jr., and E.L. Nichols Jr. 2003a. Organizational learning as a strategic resource in supply management. *Journal of Operations Management* 21: 541–556.
Hult, G.T.M., D.J. Ketchen, and S.F. Slater. 2004. Information processing, knowledge development, and strategic supply chain performance. *Academy of Management Journal* 47(2): 241–253.
Hult, G.T.M., D.J. Ketchen Jr., and S.F. Slater. 2005. Market orientation and performance: an integration of disparate approaches. *Strategic Management Journal* 26(12): 1173–1181.
Hult, G.T.M., J.A. Mena, O.C. Ferrell, and L. Ferrell. 2011. Stakeholder marketing: a definition and conceptual framework. *AMS Review* 1(1): 44–65.
Hult, G.T.M., C.C. Snow, and D. Kandemir. 2003b. The role of entrepreneurship in building cultural competitiveness in different organizational types. *Journal of Management* 29(3): 401–426.
Hunt, S.D. 2000. *A general theory of competition: resources, competences, productivity, and economic growth*. Thousand Oaks, CA: Sage.
Hunt, S.D., and R.M. Morgan. 1995. The comparative advantage theory of competition. *Journal of Marketing* 59: 1–15.
Hurley, R.F., and G.T.M. Hult. 1998. Innovation, market orientation, and organizational learning: an integration and empirical examination. *Journal of Marketing* 62: 42–54.
Hymer, S.H. 1960/1976. *The international operations of national firms: a study of direct foreign investment*. Cambridge, MA: MIT Press.
Iacobucci, D. 1996. Introduction to networks in marketing. In *Networks in marketing*, ed. D. Iacobucci. Thousand Oaks, CA: Sage.
Iacobucci, D., and N. Hopkins. 1992. Modeling dyadic interactions and networks in marketing. *Journal of Marketing Research* 24: 5–17.
Jayachandran, S., J. Gimeno, and P.R. Varadarajan. 1999. The theory of multimarket competition: a synthesis and implications for marketing strategy. *Journal of Marketing* 63: 49–66.
Jensen, M.C., and W.H. Meckling. 1976. Theory of the firm: managerial behavior, agency costs, and ownership structure. *Journal of Financial Economics* 3(4): 305–360.
Johanson, J., and J.-E. Vahlne. 2009. The Uppsala internationalization process model revisited: from liability of foreignness to liability of outsidership. *Journal of International Business Studies* 40(9): 1411–1431.
Johanson, J., and J.-E. Vahlne. 2011. Markets and networks: implications for strategy making. *Journal of the Academy of Marketing Science* 39(4): 484–491.

John, G., and T. Reve. 2010. Transaction cost analysis in marketing: looking back, moving forward. *Journal of Retailing* 86(3): 248–256.

Kahneman, D., and A. Tversky. 1979. Prospect theory: an analysis of decision under risk. *Econometrica* XLVII: 263–291.

Kast, F.E., and J.E. Rosenzweig. 1972. General systems theory: applications for organization and management. *Academy of Management Journal* 15(4): 447–465.

Keith, R.J. 1960. The marketing revolution. *Journal of Marketing* 24(3): 35–38.

Keith, J.E., D.W. Jackson, and L.A. Crosby. 1990. Effects of alternative types of influence strategies under different channel dependence structures. *Journal of Marketing* 54 (July): 30–41.

Ketchen Jr., D.J., and G.T.M. Hult. 2007a. Bridging organization theory and supply chain management: the case of best value supply chains. *Journal of Operations Management* 25(2): 573–580.

Ketchen Jr., D.J., and G.T.M. Hult. 2007b. Toward greater integration of insights from organization theory and supply chain management. *Journal of Operations Management* 25(2): 455–458.

Ketchen Jr., D.J., and G.T.M. Hult. 2007c. Bridging organization theory and supply chain management: the case of best value supply chains. *Journal of Operations Management* 25(2): 573–580.

Ketchen Jr., D.J., and G.T.M. Hult. 2011. Marketing and organization theory: opportunities for synergy. *Journal of the Academy of Marketing Science* 39(4): 481–483.

Ketchen Jr., D.J., G.T.M. Hult, and S.F. Slater. 2007. Toward greater understanding of market orientation and the resource-based view. *Strategic Management Journal* 28(9): 961–964.

Kirca, A., G.T.M. Hult, K. Roth, S.T. Cavusgil, M.Z. Perry, M.B. Akdeniz, S.Z. Deligonul, J.A. Mena, W.A. Pollitte, J.J. Hoppner, J.C. Miller, and R.C. White. 2011. Firm-specific assets, multinationality, and firm performance: a meta-analytic review and theoretical integration. *Academy of Management Journal* 54(1): 47–72.

Kirca, A.H., G.T.M. Hult, S. Deligonul, M.Z. Perry, and S.T. Cavusgil. 2012a. A multilevel examination of the drivers of firm multinationality: a meta analysis. *Journal of Management* 38 (March): 502–530.

Kirca, A.H., K. Roth, G.T.M. Hult, and S.T. Cavusgil. 2012b. The role of context in the multinationality-performance relationship: a meta-analytic review. *Global Strategy Journal* In Press.

Kogut, B., and U. Zander. 1992. Knowledge of the firm, combinative capabilities, and the replication of technology. *Organization Science* 3(3): 383–397.

Kohli, A.K., and B.J. Jaworski. 1990. Market orientation: the construct, research propositions, and managerial implications. *Journal of Marketing* 54(2): 1–18.

Li, N., W. Boulding, and R. Staelin. 2010. General alliance experience, uncertainty, and marketing alliance governance mode choice. *Journal of the Academy of Marketing Science* 38(2): 141–157.

Lucas, W.F. 1972. An overview of mathematical theory of games. *Management Science* 18: 3–19.

Lukas, B.A., J.J. Tan, and G.T.M. Hult. 2001. Strategic fit in transitional economies: the case of China's electronics industry. *Journal of Management* 27(4): 409–429.

Luo, X. 2010. Product competitiveness and beating analyst earnings target. *Journal of the Academy of Marketing Science* 38(3): 253–264.

Lusch, R.F., and S.L. Vargo. 2006. *The service-dominant logic of marketing: dialog, debate, and directions*. Armonk, NY: M.E. Sharpe, Inc.

Lusch, R.F., S.L. Vargo, and M. Tanniru. 2010. Service, value networks, and learning. *Journal of the Academy of Marketing Science* 38(1): 19–31.

Maignan, I., O.C. Ferrell, and G.T.M. Hult. 1999. Corporate citizenship: cultural antecedents and business benefits. *Journal of the Academy of Marketing Science* 27(4): 455–469.

Malshe, A., and R.S. Sohi. 2009. What makes strategy making across the sales-marketing interface more successful? *Journal of the Academy of Marketing Science* 37(4): 400–421.

Mason, E.S. 1939. Price and production policies of large-scale enterprises. *American Economic Review* 29(1): 61–74.

Mentzer, J.T., D.J. Flint, and G.T.M. Hult. 2001. Logistics service quality as a segment-customized process. *Journal of Marketing* 65(4): 82–104.

Mentzer, J.T., and G. Gundlach. 2010. Exploring the relationship between marketing and supply chain management: introduction to the special issue. *Journal of the Academy of Marketing Science* 38: 1–4.

Merz, M.A., Y. He, and S.L. Vargo. 2009. The evolving brand logic: a service-dominant logic perspective. *Journal of the Academy of Marketing Science* 37(3): 328–344.
Miner, J.B. 2003. The rated importance, scientific validity, and practical usefulness of organizational behavior theories: a quantitative review. *The Academy of Management Learning and Education* 2(3): 250–268.
Mitchell, R.K., B.R. Agle, and D.J. Wood. 1997. Toward a theory of stakeholder identification and salience: defining the principle of who and what really counts. *Academy of Management Review* 22(4): 853–886.
Moorman, C., and R.T. Rust. 1999. The role of marketing. *Journal of Marketing* 63(Special Issue): 180–197.
Morgan, R.M., and S.D. Hunt. 1994. The commitment-trust theory of relationship marketing. *Journal of Marketing* 58: 20–38.
Myers, S.C. 1977. Determinants of corporate borrowing. *Journal of Financial Economics* 5: 147–175.
Nahapiet, J., and S. Ghoshal. 1998. Social capital, intellectual capital, and the organizational advantage. *Academy of Management Review* 23(2): 242–266.
Narver, J.C., and S.F. Slater. 1990. The effect of a market orientation on business profitability. *Journal of Marketing* 54(4): 20–35.
Narver, J.C., S.F. Slater, and D.L. MacLachlan. 2000. *Total market orientation, business performance, and innovation. Report No. 00-116*. Cambridge, MA: Marketing Science Institute.
Narver, J.C., S.F. Slater, and D.L. MacLachlan. 2004. Responsive and proactive market orientation and new-product success. *Journal of Product Innovation Management* 21(5): 334–347.
von Neumann, J., and O. Morgenstern. 1944. *Theory of games and economic behavior*. Princeton, NJ: Princeton University Press.
Olson, E.M., S.F. Slater, and G.T.M. Hult. 2005. The performance implications of fit among business strategy, marketing organization structure, and strategic behavior. *Journal of Marketing* 69: 49–65.
Ouchi, W.G. 1979. A conceptual framework for the design of organizational control mechanisms. *Management Science* 25: 833–848.
Penrose, E. 1959/1995. *The theory of the growth of the firm*. Oxford: Oxford University Press.
Pfeffer, J., and G.R. Salancik. 1978. *The external control of organizations: a resource dependence perspective*. New York: Harper and Row.
Porter, M.E. 2008. The five competitive forces that shape strategy. *Harvard Business Review* 86(1): 78–97.
Porter, M.E., and M.R. Kramer. 2006. Strategy & society: the link between competitive advantage and corporate social responsibility. *Harvard Business Review* 84(12): 78–93.
Ramaswami, S.N., R.K. Srivastava, and M. Bhargava. 2009. Market-based capabilities and financial performance of firms: insights into marketing's contribution to firm value. *Journal of the Academy of Marketing Science* 37(2): 97–116.
Reimann, M., O. Schilke, and J.S. Thomas. 2010. Customer relationship management and firm performance: the mediating role of business strategy. *Journal of the Academy of Marketing Science* 38(3): 326–346.
Richey Jr., R.G., M. Tokman, and V. Dalela. 2010. Examining collaborative supply chain service technologies: a study of intensity, relationships, and resources. *Journal of the Academy of Marketing Science* 38(1): 71–89.
Rindfleisch, A., and J.B. Heide. 1997. Transaction cost analysis: past, present, and future applications. *Journal of Marketing* 61: 30–54.
Scheer, L.K., C.F. Miao, and J. Garrett. 2010. The effects of supplier capabilities on industrial customers' loyalty: the role of dependence. *Journal of the Academy of Marketing Science* 38(1): 90–104.
Schmalensee, R. 1985. Do markets differ much? *American Economic Review* 75: 341–351.
Scott, W.R. 1981. Developments in organization theory, 1960–1980. *American Behavioral Scientist* 24(3): 407–422.
Scott, W.R. 2005. Institutional theory: contributing to a theoretical research program. In *Great minds in management: the process of theory development*, ed. K.G. Smith and M.A. Hitt. Oxford: Oxford University Press.

Scott, W.R., and G.F. Davis. 2007. *Organizations and organizing: rational, natural, and open system perspectives*. Upper Saddle River, NJ: Pearson Prentice-Hall.

Selznick, P. 1957. *Leadership in administration*. New York: Harper and Row.

Shook, C.L., D.J. Ketchen Jr., G.T.M. Hult, and K.M. Kacmar. 2004. An assessment of the use of structural equation modeling in strategic management research. *Strategic Management Journal* 25(4): 397–404.

Short, J.C., D.J. Ketchen Jr., T.B. Palmer, and G.T.M. Hult. 2007. Firm, strategic group, and industry influences on performance. *Strategic Management Journal* 28(2): 147–167.

Simmel, G. 1950. Superordination and subordination and degrees of domination and freedom. In *The sociology of Georg Simmel*, ed. K.H. Wolff, 268–303. New York: The Free Press.

Simon, H.A. 1945/1997. *Administrative behavior: a study of decision-making processes in administrative organizations*. New York: The Free Press.

Simon, H.A. 1957. A behavioral model of rational choice. In *Models of man, social and rational: mathematical essays on rational human behavior in a social setting*, ed. H.A. Simon. New York: Wiley.

Slater, S.F., G.T.M. Hult, and E.M. Olson. 2007. On the importance of matching strategic behavior and target market selection to business strategy in high-tech markets. *Journal of the Academy of Marketing Science* 35(1): 5–17.

Slater, S.F., and J. Narver. 1998. Customer-led and market-oriented: let's not confuse the two. *Strategic Management Journal* 19(10): 1001–1006.

Slater, S.F., E.M. Olson, and G.T.M. Hult. 2006. The moderating influence of strategic orientation on the strategy formation capability—performance relationship. *Strategic Management Journal* 27(12): 1221–1231.

Spence, M. 1973. Job market signaling. *Quarterly Journal of Economics* 87(3): 355–374.

Spence, M. 1974. *Market signaling: informational transfer in hiring and related screening processes*. Cambridge, MA: Harvard University Press.

Srivastava, R.K., T.A. Shervani, and L. Fahey. 1999. Marketing, business processes, and shareholder value: an organizationally embedded view of marketing activities and the discipline of marketing. *Journal of Marketing* 63(Special Issue): 168–179.

Steenkamp, J-B.E.M., and I. Geyskens. 2012. Transaction cost economics and the roles of national culture: a test of hypotheses based on inglehart and hofstede. *Journal of the Academy of Marketing Science* 40 (March): 252–270.

Stiglitz, G.J. 1961. The economics of information. *Journal of Political Economy* 69(3): 213–225.

Stock, J.R., S.L. Boyer, and T. Harmon. 2010. Research opportunities in supply chain management. *Journal of the Academy of Marketing Science* 38: 32–41.

Suchman, M.C. 1995. Managing legitimacy: strategic and institutional approaches. *Academy of Management Review* 20(3): 571–610.

Taylor, F.W. 1911. *The principles of scientific management*. Sioux Falls, SD: NuVision Publications, LLC.

Teece, D.J. 2010. Forward integration and innovation: transaction costs and beyond. *Journal of Retailing* 86(3): 277–283.

Thompson, J.D. 1967. *Organizations in action*. New York: McGraw-Hill.

Thorelli, H.B. 1986. Networks: between markets and hierarchies. *Strategic Management Journal* 7(1): 37–51.

Trigeorgis, L. 1996. *Real options: managerial flexibility and strategy in resource allocation*. Cambridge, MA: MIT Press.

Tsai, K.-H., C. Chou, and J.-H. Kuo. 2008. The curvilinear relationships between responsive and proactive market orientations and new product performance: a contingent link. *Industrial Marketing Management* 37(8): 884–894.

Varadarajan, P.R. 2010. Strategic marketing and marketing strategy: domain, definition, fundamental issues and foundational premises. *Journal of the Academy of Marketing Science* 38(2): 119–140.

Vargo, S.L., and R.F. Lusch. 2004. Evolving to a new dominant logic for marketing. *Journal of Marketing* 68: 1–17.

Vargo, S.L., and R.F. Lusch. 2008. Service-dominant logic: continuing the evolution. *Journal of the Academy of Marketing Science* 36(1): 1–10.

Vorhies, D.W., and N.A. Morgan. 2005. Benchmarking marketing capabilities for sustainable competitive advantage. *Journal of Marketing* 69: 80–94.

von Bertalanffy, L. 1969. *General systems theory: foundations, development, applications.* New York: George Braziller, Inc.

Walker Jr., O.C., and R.W. Ruekert. 1987. Marketing's role in the implementation of business strategies: a critical review and conceptual framework. *Journal of Marketing* 51: 15–33.

Waluszewski, A. 1989. *Framväxten av en Mekanisk Marsateknik—en Utvecklingshistoria.* Uppsala, Sweden: Uppsala Universitet.

Webb, J.W., R.D. Ireland, M.A. Hitt, G.M. Kistruck, and L. Tihanyi. 2011. Where is the opportunity without the customer? An integration of marketing activities, the entrepreneurship process, and institutional theory. *Journal of the Academy of Marketing Science* 39(4): 537–554.

Webster, C., and A. White. 2010. Exploring the national and organizational culture mix in service firms. *Journal of the Academy of Marketing Science* 38(6): 691–703.

Webster Jr., F.E. 1992. The changing role of marketing in the corporation. *Journal of Marketing* 56: 1–17.

Webster Jr., F.E. 2009. Marketing is management. *Journal of the Academy of Marketing Science* 37(1): 20–27.

Weick, K.E. 1976. Educational organizations as loosely coupled systems. *Administrative Science Quarterly* 21: 1–19.

Wernerfelt, B. 1984. A resource-based view of the firm. *Strategic Management Journal* 5: 171–180.

Wernerfelt, B. 1997. On the nature and scope of the firm: an adjustment-cost theory. *Journal of Business* 70: 489–504.

Wernerfelt, B. 2005. Product development resources and the scope of the firm. *Journal of Marketing* 69: 15–23.

Westjohn, S.A., M.A. Arnold, P. Magnusson, S. Zdravkovic, and J.X. Zhou. 2009. Technology readiness and usage: a global-identity perspective. *Journal of the Academy of Marketing Science* 37(3): 250–265.

Wilkie, W.L., and E.S. Moore. 1999. Marketing's contributions to society. *Journal of Marketing* 63(Special Issue): 198–218.

Williamson, O.E. 1975. *Markets and hierarchies: analysis and antitrust implications.* New York: The Free Press.

Williamson, O.E., and T. Ghani. 2012. Transaction cost economics and its uses in marketing. *Journal of the Academy of Marketing Science* 40 (January): 74–85.

Wind, J.Y. 2009. Rethinking marketing: Peter Drucker's challenge. *Journal of the Academy of Marketing Science* 37(1): 28–34.

Workman Jr., J.P., C. Homburg, and K. Gruner. 1998. Marketing organization: an integrative framework of dimensions and determinants. *Journal of Marketing* 62(3): 21–41.

Yip, G.S., and G.T.M. Hult. 2012. *Total global strategy.* Upper Saddle River, NJ: Pearson Prentice-Hall.

About the Author

Dr. Hult is the Eli Broad Professor of Marketing and International Business and Director of the International Business Center (IBC) in the Eli Broad College of Business at Michigan State University. IBC has about 35 staff and student assistants and a multi-million dollar budget. He also serves as advisor to the MSU University Administration on global strategy issues and is a member of the Senior Administrators Group of MSU's Eli Broad College of Business.

Previously, he was Associate Dean in MSU's Eli Broad College of Business, a top 20 graduate business school in the United States (*Forbes* 2011, *BusinessWeek* 2011) with top specialties in international business and supply chain management. The Broad College of Business has roughly 5,600 students (approximately 4,800 undergraduates and 800 graduate students). MSU is a member of the Association of American Universities.

Dr. Hult has been the Executive Director of the Academy of International Business (with some 3,200 members in about 80 countries) and President of the AIB Foundation since 2004. Previously, Hult served as Vice President of International Activities for the American Marketing Association and as a Board Member of AMA's Global Interest Group. He is on the Board of the International Trade Center of Mid-Michigan, The Economic Club of Greater Lansing, the Global Business Club of Mid-Michigan, and the Jagdish and Madhuri Sheth Foundation.

Dr. Hult's specialty areas are in international marketing strategy, global strategy, and supply chain management. He is one of the world's leading authorities at the intersection of international business and supply chain management. His most recent book is *Total Global Strategy* (2012) with George Yip (published by Pearson Prentice-Hall).

According to a ranking by Thomson Reuters, Professor Hult was the 75th most-cited "scientist in economics and business" in the world for 1997–2007. His research has been cited about 10,000 times per Google Scholar (three-quarters of the citations coming since 2007). Hult has published 46 articles in top journals including *Academy of Management Journal, Strategic Management Journal, Journal of International Business Studies, Journal of Marketing, Journal of the Academy of Marketing*

Science, *Journal of Retailing*, *Journal of Management*, *Journal of Operations Management*, *Decision Sciences*, and *IEEE Transactions on Engineering Management*, and he has published more than 100 total journal articles.

In fundraising, Dr. Hult has been responsible for raising more than $11 million for MSU since 2001 and more than $3 million for AIB since 2004. He is an elected Fellow of the Academy of International Business and Editor-in-Chief of the *Journal of the Academy of Marketing Science*, which is ranked second among marketing journals in the 2010 impact scores. A dual citizen of Sweden and the United States, Tomas Hult has been residing in the United States since 1987 and has been a professor at Michigan State University since January 2001. Prior to MSU, he was at Florida State University from 1996 to 2000, serving as Director of FSU's International Business Programs.

More information about Dr. Tomas Hult can be found at http://global.broad.msu.edu/hult.

MIX
Papier aus verantwortungsvollen Quellen
Paper from responsible sources
FSC® C105338
FSC
www.fsc.org

If you have any concerns about our products,
you can contact us on
ProductSafety@springernature.com

In case Publisher is established outside the EU,
the EU authorized representative is:
Springer Nature Customer Service Center GmbH
Europaplatz 3, 69115 Heidelberg, Germany

Printed by Libri Plureos GmbH
in Hamburg, Germany